D1345765

PELICAN BOOKS

Words or Blows

Racial Attitudes in Australia

Lorna Lippmann is Research Officer at the Centre for
Research into Aboriginal Affairs, Monash University. She is a
graduate in Arts of Melbourne University and has been
actively involved in Aboriginal affairs for the last fifteen
years. Her research work has taken her to most Australian
States, to Indian reservations in the United States and to
Maori areas of New Zealand. She is author of
To Achieve Our Country: Australia and the Aborigines,
Melbourne, 1970, and of numerous papers and articles
on racial attitudes and Aboriginal affairs.

Words or Blows

Racial Attitudes in Australia

Lorna Lippmann

Penguin Books

Penguin Books Ltd, Harmondsworth,
Middlesex, England
Penguin Books Australia Ltd, Ringwood,
Victoria, Australia

First published 1973
Copyright © Lorna Lippmann, 1973

Printed in Australia for
Penguin Books Australia Ltd
at The Dominion Press, Blackburn, Victoria
Set in Intertype Times

Contents

ink 4-11-84
301. 451
L 76 w

Tables and Figures

Acknowledgements

I would like to thank the Aboriginal people of the four country towns, who consistently display more tolerance than they receive. The assistance of many officials and other citizens of the towns is also warmly acknowledged.

The study was only made possible by grants from the Office of Aboriginal Affairs and the Department of Anthropology and Sociology, Monash University, to whom I am indebted.

For their most helpful comments on the manuscript of this book I would like to express appreciation to Dr E. M. Eggleston, Professor C. M. Tatz and Dr F. Thompson; and for their assistance with the extensive typing involved to Mrs M. Slutzkin and Mrs S. Stevenson.

LORNA LIPPMANN

To Walter, Davina and Lenora, but for whose assistance this book would have been written in half the time

'Power concedes nothing without demand. It never did and it never will. Find out what any people will quietly submit to and you have found out the exact measure of injustice and wrong which will be imposed upon them, and these will continue till they are resisted with either words or blows, or with both.'

FREDERICK DOUGLASS ('Father' of the Black Panther Movement, U.S.A.), August 1857.

Part One

The Setting

Introduction

It is only in comparatively recent years that Australians have become aware that a racial situation has grown up in this country which, though involving in the main only some 150,000 Aborigines and part-Aborigines in a total population of 13,000,000, is rapidly becoming more pressing and more urgent as the disparity in living standards between black and white grows greater and the voice of the black minority becomes stronger.

This situation bears only slight resemblance to that of the United Kingdom, where the coloured population consists of fairly recent immigrants whose presence in industrial areas has served to accentuate the shortcomings of the major society. Where there is already inadequate accommodation and employment, the temptation will be great to vent frustration on newcomers who are obviously different in appearance and culture. The reverse has been the case in Australia: Aborigines* have always been with us and we are used to ignoring them. Their smallness of number, residence in remote areas and considerable cultural differences ensure that most white urban dwellers have no direct contact with them.

Nor is the position of the blacks in the United States directly comparable: a coloured minority who have sufficient numbers, resources and organization to disrupt the major society are in a far stronger position than are a small, dispersed and almost powerless group – their Australian counterparts. The New Zealand race situation also bears considerable differences from our own. The indigenous

* The words Aborigine and Aboriginal will be used throughout, unless otherwise stated, to denote both Aborigines of the full descent and part-Aborigines.

11

people, the Maoris, were never as totally defeated as were the Aborigines, never so driven to distant areas. Though disparities between Maori and white undoubtedly exist in health, education, housing and the like, there has always been a recognition and at least a partial acceptance of the Maori and his culture into the total society.

In one sense, then, the situation of the Aborigine is different from all other. Not alone has he been totally defeated, but also totally ignored; his has been a background presence which has only recently obtruded on to the white consciousness. Yet, in another sense, the position of all these coloured communities is similar, being part of a race-relations pattern where, as a result of specific historical events, the behaviour of two or more social groups towards each other has gradually become part of a habit, enabling response to take place with minimum effort. Being an integral part of the social whole, race relations are determined by an interplay of factors, economic, geographic, political and historic, working simultaneously on a multitude of individual personalities.

This study of four Australian towns relates principally to the place of part-Aboriginal urban dwellers in predominantly white communities and attempts to show what it is like to be an Aborigine in a country town today. But the first six chapters are concerned with all the many factors which have determined the setting in which the Aborigine lives. What causes the inter-group tensions which bedevil not only Australia but so many parts of the world today? Are these causes social, economic or psychological or, perhaps, a combination of all three? The attitudes of our citizens of the country towns have unconsciously been influenced by a host of diverse and often contradictory factors, which have achieved a gradual but decisive change in public attitudes since the early days of European settlement; and that change has been epitomized by the historians, the mass media and the public opinion polls. Pronouncements by politicians and actions by administrators will in part be a reaction to both racist and anti-racist pressure groups and in part to the exigencies of the economic and political situation.

Despite a continuous spate of news items concerning racial matters, there is still remarkably little known of a precise, factual nature of the aspirations or prospects of black Australians. The belief is still current that the various government agencies dealing with Aboriginal affairs must, overall, be effecting improvements, with more money to spend now than ever before and more trained personnel to spend it; even though for generations these agencies have proven themselves ill-equipped to deal with what to Aborigines appears a hopeless and worsening socio-economic situation. Since charity has compounded Aboriginal degradation in the past, would bigger and better handouts equalize their position? These have been tried by the Northern Territory Social Welfare administration in recent years in the form of more adequate and slightly better housing; but to no avail. The social disintegration of Aboriginal groups in northern and central areas is increasing, among a people purposeless and bereft: their culture rendered meaningless and themselves passed by as permanent outsiders.

Should Aboriginal 'welfare', then, be eliminated altogether, under the pretence that this would end discrimination? But this would be to compound inequality further, since those who enter the race well behind the starting barrier cannot hope to compete on equal terms. In New South Wales during the 1960s government policy was to leave Aboriginal reserves without support and to counsel the inhabitants to move to other areas, seemingly on the basis that if the misery were wider spread it would not be such an affront to white eyes. But the policy did not, could not work, because many of the reserve residents were simply not equipped by education or experience to live in a competitive society, which at any time might show prejudice against them. They chose emotional security and continued

to inhabit the reserves in the shacks and shanties which fulfilled the expectation of the white racist as to Aboriginal
inadequacy.

Both these 'solutions', though frequently tried, have just
as frequently been found wanting. Basic lack of confidence
in Aboriginal ability has prevented their being allocated
resources, both economic and educational, which would
allow control of their own affairs and bring in its train a
fair share of political power. Behind the periodic revamping
of the bureaucracy controlling Aboriginal affairs lurk the
recurring suspicions of our forefathers: 'But in ability, are
they *really* equal?' In any case 'welfare' is cheaper and less
threatening to whites than fair shares.

To dub white Australians 'racist' or 'racialist' (the ideology and practice of race superiority) advances nothing.
Indeed, there is a very real danger that it will enhance intolerance. Where all are guilty, no one is responsible; where
all are prejudiced no one is to blame. A corporate feeling
of guilt becomes almost cosy as a means of group integration, and certainly requires less intellectual effort than does
careful reappraisal. Nor will Aborigines be assisted by the
heartfelt cry that it is all the fault of the system: capitalism
or bureaucratic rule. It is hard to argue with the contention
that racism is an inherent part of capitalism: a political system which permits a permanent bottom rung of those who
are ill-housed, ill-fed, ill-educated, will surely have that
rung at least partly filled by a black minority. But if capitalism were to disappear from Australia overnight, attitudes
towards race would not so quickly change. The same people
with the same deeply rooted prejudices would remain and
with them, doubt as to Aboriginal equality. There is ample
evidence from non-capitalist countries to prove the point.

Consideration of black–white relationships in Australia
both past and present, particularly of their less comforting
aspects, may enable us as white Australians to slough off
some of our ingrained ethnocentricity and heed the cry of
'White Man, Listen!' which is being made by black Australians with ever-increasing urgency.

Chapter One

Race Relations

The findings of biologists and psychologists over the decades have not supported the theory of any group's innate superiority over all others, though there are undoubtedly intergroup differences in ability and mental development, not all of which may be explicable on cultural grounds. In spite of this knowledge, racism has scarcely diminished and an increasing number of social scientists have turned to an examination of its causes and functions so that from these universal truths may come a better understanding of the inter-group friction which seems to have become a permanent and threatening feature of present-day society. Once such abrasive sets of behaviour become part of the total social structure they achieve a personal and social utility, a force of their own, and are not easily altered, even where outward circumstances have changed.

In the country towns we are to examine, though the economic position of Aborigines is not as deeply depressed as once it was, they are nevertheless, as a group, still on the bottom socio-economic rung; and though discriminatory legislation has been abolished in the two States in question, Victoria and New South Wales, the results of legal inequalities have clearly had their effect on both Aboriginal and white attitudes, while discriminatory administration has not yet disappeared. A small, economically depressed minority of distinctive appearance who have been traditional targets of racialism must be ideal marks for individual aggression and, by the very fact of their cultural differences, a bolster to social cohesion and feelings of comfortable superiority among the white community. Yet there is no need for resigned acceptance of the ingrained character of racism in any given area. Certain types of educational programme[1] have been shown to effect positive change; and anti-racist legislation will provide the social foundation for the alteration of group attitudes by creating or clarifying rights and then enabling them to be protected or enforced. Once laws were changed to enable Aborigines to vote and to drink alcohol, these were accepted as right and proper by the majority of whites.

The possible causes of racial tensions have been occupying the minds of social scientists for generations. The early social anthropologists of the late nineteenth century came to use Darwinism as a basis for speculation about race. Their best-known member, Paul Broca, accepted as fact an inexorable historic development towards the triumph of a superior group. One of the first Americans to theorize about race relations (in the 1930s) was W. Lloyd Warner[2] who saw the white population of the United States as divided into classes, the members of which were free to work their way to the top, while blacks faced an impenetrable barrier of caste, or fixed social positioning, which transcended both income and education. Karl Marx, whose influence was profound in this as in other fields, had stated that there was an economic basis to all man's activities, thoughts and desires, and thus racism was a strategy of the ruling class to justify ascendancy. O. C. Cox,[3] an American black Marxist, disputed Warner's caste theory because the so-called American 'castes' were not tied to specific occupations, as they were in India, nor was there any general agreement as to their exact position in the social hierarchy. The black worker, to Cox, was a pawn in the conflict of classes, to be used and exploited by one white class or another, and always to be labelled as inferior. But this does not really explain why black workers should be more exploited than whites; and Robin Williams[4] was later to prove that a city's level of unemployment or of income is not directly connected with discrimination. In fact, areas of high unemployment and low average income are sometimes found to be comparatively tolerant.

Despite arguments against it, Cox's conflict theory was revived at a later date by Stanley Lieberson[5] who considered that the critical problem in inter-group contact which would decide future racial attitudes was each group's desire to maintain a social order in accord with its lifeways prior to such contact. One of his supporters in this theory, John Rex, believed that it was also the element of competition which was at the root of a racist situation between two groups, and the resultant aggression became channelled into dislike of the competitor, who was therefore seen as evil and 'inferior'.[6]

Whereas Marx and his followers had been convinced that economic factors were of overwhelming importance in race relations, Max Weber[7] challenged this view by insisting on the importance of the ethos or system of belief as the major influence. While conceding the role of economic class he added other factors, those of status or prestige and also of power, or ability to control. The importance of ideals was carried a step further by Gunnar Myrdal[8] in a monumental work which stressed the discrepancy between the American creed, based on the Bill of Rights, and everyday American practice; a discrepancy made acceptable by the invention of myths to prove black 'inferiority'. His writings in many ways had a profound influence on racial thinking in the United States, though he was criticized by Robert Merton[9] for over-simplifying. Merton felt that Myrdal had omitted a third factor in the formation of race attitudes, namely, the beliefs of the individual, who did not necessarily feel in his heart that all his co-citizens were entitled to 'life, liberty and the pursuit of happiness'. The social psychologist John Harding[10] maintained that a prejudiced attitude implied a departure from no fewer than three ideal 'norms' (or what ought to be): the norm of rationality, the norm of justice and what he called the norm of 'human-heartedness'. But this still leaves unanswered the question of why social norms are accepted by some individuals and rejected by others who live within the same society and are subjected to the same social influences. One explanation was given by Frank Westie[11] who wrote of two flatly contradictory American 'creeds' in operation, one of which enjoined the brotherhood of man, while the other insisted that one ought to be prejudiced and one ought to discriminate, since this had been the practice for centuries past. He also discovered, in his studies of race relations, that very often lip-service is paid to the ideals of the Christian-democratic creed where its practice is not supported: many who rejoiced in the concept of equality did not want to eat at the same table as a black person.

The social psychologists in general, however, tackled the question of departure from norms on an individual rather than on a social level and saw racism as fulfilling a function for the individual personality rather than for society as a whole. Sigmund Freud had expounded the theory that the antipathies which people feel towards strangers are in reality an expression of self-love, while one of his followers, John Dollard,[12] views race prejudice as the outward manifestation of early frustration which has resulted in aggression. Since this aggression is not acceptable in personal relationships, it gets diverted into scapegoating, or blaming a particular group for all that seems wrong in the social environment. His view was supported by Bruno Bettelheim,[13] who regarded stereotyping as an act of weakness, a defence mechanism to guard the ego of the individual.

A further study of race prejudice considered from the individual viewpoint was the classic, *The Authoritarian Personality*,[14] where the authors have attempted to describe general personality characteristics of highly prejudiced people, proving that authoritarian personalities have a tendency towards group prejudice. But there is no reason to suppose that one country town in Australia will have a higher proportion of authoritarian personalities than another, although the degree of measurable prejudice in different towns might vary considerably. Similarly, studies of white Southerners in the United States have not found evidence of a greater prevalence of authoritarianism in areas noted for their high degree of prejudice; while the steady decline in hostile attitudes towards Jews and blacks, also in the United States, is unlikely to stem from a diminution of frustration or a decrease in the proportion of authoritarians.

Yet another Freudian, Erich Fromm,[15] combines the individual with the social approach. He theorizes that individual identity is only attained by the young person when he discards the family ties which had given him early security. His resultant feeling of aloneness may produce anxiety and fear which he projects on to another group. Race prejudice will then become an attempt to create an individual identity through negative indentification. That is to say, if the group with negative characteristics is one to which the individual does not belong, he will automatically feel himself to be a member of another, superior group. This harks back to previous sociologists who were aware of the cohesive function of group prejudice, its ability to give a feeling of 'togetherness'. Antagonism may take on a positive and integrating role[16] and racial superiority will emerge as a characteristic expression of that solidarity which springs from man's innate gregariousness and . . . serves the magnificent purpose of elevating the ego.'[17] There has been psychiatric agreement on the stabilizing, aggression-absorbing function of racism,[18] which Talcott Parsons had previously dubbed 'pattern maintenance and tension management'. Parsons[19] had formulated one of the most influential theories of social stratification, by pointing out that the system of social classes was modified by the presence of ethnic groups tending to form their own strata, independent of the whole.

Despite these many and sometimes conflicting viewpoints, there has been a fair measure of concensus on the theory that majority–minority relationships are only a slightly exaggerated form of the fixed status and limited mobility of many class systems; that they are in large measure status and power relations; and that race prejudice is a manifestation of the social position of two or more groups.[20] As a Japanese social scientist has rightly observed, 'How a person is treated does not depend so much upon what he is as upon the manner in which he is defined.'[21] The Englishman, Michael Banton, points out that those who sought to defend ethnic inequality formerly turned to biology; when biological racist theories were discredited, they turned to psychology; when it was discovered that most tests of mental capacity tended to have a cultural bias towards the middle-class white, they turned to anthropology; and there discovered the comforting theory that the poor are apt to transmit certain cultural characteristics (usually considered undesirable) to their offspring. All of which proves that, given prejudice, one can always find some scientific theory which appears to give it support. But Banton maintains that ethical and political considerations, not the theories of social scientists or the prejudice of individuals, determine the poverty of black minorities in white societies.[22] The low social position of a minority, after all, stems from its economic and political powerlessness which, in turn, results from unequal access to community resources.

Yet another explanation of the formation of race relations has come from a group of sociologists[23] who have found that in a modern mass society the common ideals instilled early in life may later change considerably in order to accord with the norms of the group to which the individual belongs; and that behaviour in an industrialized society is in practice controlled by social institutions and organized interest groups.

Many of these theories do not in fact conflict, but complement each other. The black and white citizens of the country towns will be influenced by many different factors, their racial attitudes affected by a variety of causes. Their views will not be the same as those of their fathers because social attitudes in general towards race have changed dramatically, even in the last half-century, and it is to this change that we now turn our attention.

Notes

1. CARNIE, J. M., 'The Contribution of School Geography to the Improvement of International Understanding', unpublished M.A. thesis, London, 1963; WAKATOMA, M. A., 'An Experimental Study of the Geography of South Africa with Special Reference to its Effects upon the Attitudes of English Children towards Africans', unpublished M.A. thesis, London, 1957; SARNOFF, J. and KATZ, D., 'Ego Defence and Attitude Change', *Human Relations*, vol. 9, 1956, pp. 27–45; and many others.

2. WARNER, W. LLOYD, 'American Class and Caste', *American Journal of Sociology*, vol. 42, September 1936, pp. 234–7.

3. COX, O. C., *Caste, Class and Race*, New York, 1959.

4. WILLIAMS, ROBIN M. Jun., *Strangers Next Door*, New Jersey, 1964.

5. LIEBERSON, STANLEY, 'A Societal Theory of Race and Ethnic Relations', in MACK, R. (ed.), *Race, Class and Power*, New York, 1968, pp. 42–52.

6. REX, JOHN, *Race Relations in Sociological Theory*, London, 1970.

7. WEBER, MAX, *The Protestant Ethic and the Spirit of Capitalism*, New York, 1930.

8. MYRDAL, G., *An American Dilemma*, 4th edition, New York, 1944.

9. MERTON, ROBERT K., 'Discrimination and the American Creed', in MACIVER, R. M. (ed.), *Discrimination and National Welfare*, New York, 1949.

10. HARDING, JOHN, *et al.*, 'Prejudice and Ethnic Relations,' in LINDZEY, G. (ed.), *Handbook of Social Psychology*, vol. 2, Cambridge, 1954, pp. 1021–61.

11. WESTIE, FRANK R., 'The American Dilemma: An Empirical Test', in MACK, R. (ed.), *Race, Class and Power*, 2nd ed., New York, 1968.

12. DOLLARD, J., 'Hostility and Fear in Social Life', *Social Forces*, vol. 17, 1938, pp. 15–26.

13. BETTELHEIM, B., 'The Dynamism of Anti-Semitism in Gentile and Jew', *Journal of Abnormal Psychology*, vol. 32, 1947, pp. 153–68.

14. ADORNO, T. W., *et al.*, *The Authoritarian Personality*, New York, 1950; and CHRISTIE, R. and JAHODA, M. (eds.), *Studies in Scope and Method of 'The Authoritarian Personality'*, Glencoe, Illinois, 1954.

15. FROMM, E., *The Fear of Freedom*, London, 1960.

16. SIMMEL, GEORG, *Conflict and the Web of Group Affiliations*, Glencoe, Illinois, 1955, p. 18.

17. As quoted in ROSE, PETER I., *The Subject is Race*, New York, 1968.

18. KOVEL, JOEL, *White Racism, A Psychohistory*, London, 1970.

19. PARSONS, T., *Essays in Sociological Theory*, Glencoe, Illinois, 1954.

20. WESTIE, F. R., 'Race and Ethnic Relations' in FARIS, R. E. L. (ed.), *Handbook of Modern Sociology*, Chicago, 1966; HIMES, J. S., 'The Functions of Racial Conflict', *Social Forces*, vol. 45, no. 1; ROSE, PETER I., op. cit.; BLUMER, H., 'Recent Research on the Racial Problems of the United States of America', *International Social Science Bulletin*, vol. 10, pp. 403–47.

21. SHIBUTANI, TAMOTSU and KWAN, KIAN M., *Ethnic Stratification*, New York, 1965, p. 27.

22. BANTON, M., 'The Concept of Racism', in ZUBAIDA, S. (ed.), *Race and Racialism*, London, 1970.

23. LOHMAN, J. D. and REITZES, D. C., 'Deliberately Organized Groups and Racial Behaviour', *American Sociological Review*, vol. 19, pp. 343–4; BLUMER, H., op. cit.; MILLS, C. W., *The Power Elite*, New York, 1959; SHILS, E. A., 'Mass Society and Its Culture', in *Culture for the Millions*, Princeton, New Jersey, 1961.

Chapter Two

Australia – A Racist Country?

The treatment of Aborigines by the early white settlers of Australia has by now been too well documented to require detailed repetition.[1] The clashes between black and white over life-giving lands inevitably ended in Aborigines being swept back into remote territory unwanted by the new settlers, and rapidly decimated by homicide and disease; their social cohesion gone, their spiritual unity destroyed.

Accounts of individual and group acts of cruelty abound. Dame Mary Gilmour recalled how, as a child, she was staying on her grandfather's property and saw an Aboriginal man and his wife bathing in the river. A passing white settler, on his way home from an unsuccessful rabbiting expedition, raised his gun and shot the woman, for no reason other than for 'sport'. When the husband, with a cry of anguish, went to his wife's assistance, he also was shot and killed. In Tasmania, in the race wars which ended in Aboriginal extermination, black children were taken from their parents to become a source of cheap labour. In all parts of the country they were as common a target for bands of hunters as were kangaroos, and were regarded as a similar sort of pest, with their frequent raids on sheep and cattle to replace the wild game now beyond their reach, and their sporadic fighting to retain traditional lands. The settler reprisals which followed often wiped out the whole Aboriginal population of an area.

Nor did the inhumanity cease after the Select Committee on Aborigines, set up by the British House of Commons in 1837, had recommended Protectors for their defence. The 'protective' laws were in themselves highly discriminatory and, under them, callousness became legalized and codified. The Protectors, being the legal guardians of Aboriginal children, could take them from their parents and send them to institutions; adults could be ordered on to reserves and held there indefinitely; areas, such as whole towns, could be declared prohibited to Aborigines and permission had to be obtained before an Aborigine was allowed to marry. All this took place, not in the distant past, but within the memory of very many who are alive today. Permission to marry in Western Australia, for example, had to be obtained until as late as 1954; in the same State, neck-chains were being used to bring criminal suspects into town up till 1958; while in Queensland in the 1950s Aborigines were sometimes tied to trees and left overnight as punishment (without trial) for alleged misdemeanours. The Darwin *Northern Standard* in 1930 was still supporting shooting out of hand for Aboriginal miscreants (which, in practice, included possible miscreants) since the exigencies of the frontier situation, they proclaimed, did not warrant legal procedures. As Charles Rowley has said, 'Murder, rape and cruelty have been commonplace over wide areas and long periods',[2] with Aborigines soon fulfilling the white expectation of degradation and hopelessness.

To contend that this treatment was a manifestation of the cruelties of a barbarous age would be an over-simplification. Cruelty there was in plenty, coupled with total disregard for Aborigines as sentient human beings, but these attitudes stemmed from a deeply entrenched belief in the superiority of white man over black, reinforced by many of the religious and philosophic concepts of the time, and by the needs of the local economic and political situation.

After the Treaty of Paris of 1763 between England and France, England became the supreme colonial and (later) industrial power and required markets for her secondary products and raw materials for her manufactures. The Australian grasslands proved suitable for the production of merino wool and ever-widening areas of land were needed by the settlers to meet these and other demands. Although guerrilla warfare continued for a considerable period it was always the black Australian who fared worse since he was, from the outset, technically inferior, and soon became numerically so. In the Aboriginal society there were no economic surpluses nor clearly defined lines of command from headman downwards (as there were with the New Zealand Maoris or many of the peoples of the Pacific), nor were there settled villages to which to retreat and regroup. Furthermore, the Europeans, with all their sophisticated armoury, were the first large-scale invaders with whom Aborigines had ever had to deal. It was not surprising then, that their showing on the battlefield was less impressive than that of their New Zealand counterparts and that, as a result, they earned no treaties or rights to specific tracts of land.

The 'cult of indifference' towards Aborigines was engendered not only by their powerlessness and disarray but also by the religious beliefs current at the time. Christianity had become an integral part of the ethic of colonialism, since its function was seen as the suppression of native cults and the conversion of the black man to the spiritual values of the one true faith. Charles Darwin's biological theory of natural selection and the survival of the fittest had been distorted to reinforce racist philosophies: the less fit or technically primitive peoples of the world were destined to die out or assimilate with the stronger (despite the fact that Darwin himself had stated that man's sympathies should be extended 'to the men of all nations and races'). Though the driving forces were nationalist and economic, it was a simple matter to construct theories suggesting that it was a duty to rule the weak. Kipling's *Recessional* was a latter-day revival of Aristotle's attempt to defend the vested interests of racial exploitation in terms of divinely ordained inequalities. The 'barbarians' of the ancient world were now the coloured peoples, 'half devil and half child', poor Calibans to be entrusted to modern Prosperos such as Cecil Rhodes. This was linked with a belief in the perfectibility of mankind, based increasingly on economic prowess and technical excellence, a belief which has been recurrent throughout history.

The English philosopher David Hume had written in 1770 of the natural inferiority of coloured people, since they were 'devoid of manufactures, of arts and of sciences'[3] and all over Europe scholars were turning their attention to the obvious differences between groups and trying to rationalize the exploitative nature of imperialism. Friedrich List, a prominent German economist in the early nineteenth century, believed that European peoples were eminently qualified and designated by Providence to colonize and civilize wild or uninhabited countries. But it is in France of the 1850s that we discover the most important systematization of racist historical theory in the *Essay on the Inequality of Human Races* of Count Joseph Arthur de Gobineau, a member of the minor French nobility who was distressed by the exclusion of his class from government. Convinced that this was a symptom of European decadence, de Gobineau sought an explanation. The downfall of civilization stems from miscegenation between races; the black race is distinguished by its animality and limited intellect but is full of energy and will. The yellow is also quite incapable of building or enhancing a civilization. Needless to say it is the white race from which stems 'everything great, noble and fruitful'. Later in the nineteenth century that colourful Englishman, Houston Stewart Chamberlain, son of an English admiral and eventually son-in-law of Richard Wagner, contended that the differences between the races were so evident that their inequality was a matter of factual observation. A contemporary English writer, Philip Mason,[4] has suggested that differences in national character have much to do with the unequal susceptibilities of societies to prejudice and that the north European Protestant peoples' sensitivity to racial differences has roots in their common character as shaped by traditions, family institutions and histories which they do not share with the peoples of southern and eastern Europe. This acute awareness of even minor cultural differences lends itself to an unease, a distaste, even an aversion towards those who are by appearance obviously different. This is too sweeping a generalization to be provable in detail but it adds an interesting sidelight to the Australian situation and might possibly account for the fact that de Gobineau societies sprang up all over Germany while France remained almost impervious to his racist writings.

Thus the early English settlers arrived in Australia with strong philosophic, religious and economic sanction for their feelings of ineffable superiority which were only deepened by the distance from Europe: Australia saw herself as a European jewel set in an alien sea. Geographic proximity to Asia, far from engendering feelings of common interest, enhanced among the early settlers the consciousness of being British. Unpleasant reminders of the lack of cultural unity, such as Aborigines and Asians, were reviled, scorned or simply treated as non-existent.

Only gradually has the realization come that our self-image as a purely Western nation, inconveniently situated, is no longer tenable. Since 1788 we have been a multi-cultural society. The close trade link with the United Kingdom has diminished and will continue to do so with the latter's entry into the European Economic Community. Strategic ties to the United States also show signs of weakening while trade with our Asian neighbours increases steadily year by year and is accompanied by pressure for some increase in Asian immigration. Moreover, the constant discrimination which Aborigines have experienced since the coming of the white man to Australia is currently being placed under strain by the reality of an increasingly industrialized society with its need for a trained, interchangeable labour force; by the high levels of educational and economic aspiration throughout the community which must have its effect on black as well as white; and the commonality of cultural and behavioural patterns which such a society brings in its train. In the southern parts of Australia especially, where part-Aborigines predominate over

Words or Blows

Aborigines of the full descent, the number of social values accepted by all citizens far exceed those where differences occur between the racial groups; and so the black demand is for standard housing, regular employment, legal and health services – all facilities which are taken for granted in the white society.

Notes

1. Changes in official policy and in legislation regarding Aborigines have been dealt with in LIPPMANN, LORNA, *To Achieve Our Country: Australia and the Aborigines*, Melbourne, 1970.
2. ROWLEY, C. D., *Aboriginal Policy and Practice*, vol. 1, *The Destruction of Aboriginal Society*, Canberra, 1970, p. 7. For a detailed study of black–white relationships see the trilogy under this title.
3. HUME, DAVID, *Essays and Treaties on Several Subjects*, London, 1770, vol. 1, p. 329.
4. MASON, PHILIP, 'An Essay on Racial Tension', *Royal Institute of International Affairs*, London, 1954, pp. 37–42.

Chapter Three

A Changing Viewpoint

It would scarcely be fair to judge the historians of, say, fifty years ago by the mores of our own time. They exemplify in their accounts of the dealings of the early white settlers with Aborigines, Pacific Islanders and Asians a change in philosophic outlook and public attitude towards people of different race. The earlier historians glossed over the considerable prejudice of most of the British settlers towards non-Europeans, accepted their false self-justification and often ignored the very existence of Aborigines. But gradually there has come an awareness that both minority and majority societies are best served by facing the reality of events (even where these have been unpalatable) and explaining, though not necessarily justifying, their cause. And so with time Australian histories have become more objective, more humane and less xenophobic.

A glance at some of these race histories also fulfils the secondary purpose of providing direct evidence of the racial attitudes which were current throughout the nineteenth and into the twentieth centuries and which were crystallized under the *Immigration Restriction Act* of 1901. One of the earliest post-graduate studies of this founding of the 'White Australia' policy was that of Myra Willard a half-century ago.

She accepted the official reasons for the policy of restricted non-European immigration (that it was to avoid the largely economic problems of cheap labour) while at the same time extensively quoting racist sentiments which *per se* disprove the contention. The Chinese migrants were variously referred to by the colonists as 'a swarm of human locusts', a 'sore that would grow into a plague-spot' and (by the goldminers) as 'an inferior Asiatic race ... that proved able to mine so successfully'.[1] Alfred Deakin in 1901 had maintained that only whites would be fit to live under the new constitution, so broad and liberal would it be. [!] In the face of these and a host of similar racist pronouncements, Willard comes to the remarkable conclusion that the politicians of the day were not actuated by any idea of the inferiority of the excluded peoples, but by the fact that the latter were 'unfit to exercise political rights and incompetent to fulfil political duties'. In other words, they *were* inferior.

Willard was inaccurate in her assessment. In the drafting of the Federal Constitution there had been considerable discussion as to whether something on the lines of the United States Fourteenth Amendment should be included: 'No State shall make or enforce any law which shall abridge the privileges or immunities of citizens of the United States.' But, after considerable debate, Australians were denied constitutional guarantees against deprivation of life, liberty or property without the process of law because of the uncomfortable realization that this would invalidate the Victorian factory legislation which discriminated against the Chinese, or that of Western Australia which prevented Asians or Africans from obtaining a miner's right. Presumably, also (though this does not appear to have been specifically considered by the members of the constitution Convention) a host of discriminatory State laws concerning Aborigines would have been thrown into awkward juxtaposition.

At about the same time came the quaintly-titled *Non-Britishers in Australia*[2] which aimed to show the contribution of our society of the 2 per cent of foreigners. Included in these 'foreigners' are the Aborigines who, despite the author's awareness that they are British subjects, are apparently not really British, being black. Lyng states that Aborigines were easily conquered because of their 'incoherence [*sic*], deficiency in racial pride and their extreme primitiveness'.[3] However, the author points out that it is wrong to assume that Aborigines have nothing to give to the white race since their ability to track and to procure food and water had saved many a pioneer's life. It was doubtful, Lyng continues, if in the north the pastoral industry could be carried on without them, and due acknowledgement is given to the contribution of the part-Aborigine to a variety of occupations in the urban workforce. The conclusion is a plea for a racially mixed population in Australia – Mediterraneans, Alpines, Nordics and even coloured peoples – providing they are assimilable.[4]

In 1942 P.M.C. (later Sir Paul) Hasluck published *Black Australians*,[5] a study of the seventy years of contact between white settlers and indigenes from 1829, when the Swan River was colonized, to the end of the century when the British government surrendered control of Aborigines to the Western Australian government. Though it deals with only one State, the sorry tale epitomizes black–white relationships over the whole country for this period. The first Mounted Police Corps, with a Superintendent of Natives at its head, was formed with the aim of protecting and at the same time controlling Aborigines. But its real nature in practice, as an escort for mail and settlers, was to give protection *against* rather than *of* Aborigines. Legal 'pacification' was left to police who pounced on the camps of criminal suspects and brought back as many as they could encompass on a chain. Trial was followed by exile on Rottnest Island or a flogging and gaoling locally. Arbitrary shooting was not uncommon, either by police or settlers, and was usually reported as action in self-defence, to prevent escape, or even to save property. Hasluck's laconic comment is that even if the police sometimes 'killed blacks a shade too zealously, for the most part they did their work with a patience, forbearance and sense of honour that did credit to their force' though he admits that, as late as the 1890s, 'the court was a process by which [the Aborigine] was sent to gaol; not a place where he defended himself against an unproved charge.'

Though Hasluck seems unaware of the fact, *Black Australians* contained sufficient evidence of racism to stir the national conscience. But the national conscience was not to be thus easily stirred. The book was issued in a very limited edition, made little impression except among scholars, and the author's judgement was accepted that the 'taming' of the natives had been rather rigorous at times but was, on the whole, reasonable and just.

From the 1930s onward anthropologists continued with their researches into the traditional society, emphasizing its complex social organization, deep spirituality, co-operation with Nature and the dignity and worth of the individuals of whom it was comprised. Indeed it was one of these anthropologists, A. P. Elkin, who contributed much to the introduction of the 1939 official policy of assimilation which, though leaving a great deal to be desired, was still an improvement on the previous aim of segregation. But the public impact of such writings was not great, unless they had been immediately preceded by some anti-Aboriginal outrage.

The early historians had largely ignored the Aboriginal contribution to Australia's national life, either before or after Cook's landing. Manning Clark considers that they had developed a culture but not a civilization of their own and had been unable to make 'the transition from barbarism'[6] without the assistance of the white man. He refers to 'the revenge of the aborigine [sic] against the white man for stealing the land [which] brought great hardship and suffering' (of course to the white man). The latter gradually became disgusted by the Aborigine's personal habits, indolence and inability to raise himself out of his 'material squalor'. The Short History was still being written largely from the point of view of the steadfast pioneers who were perpetually besieged by savages; but Clark does point out, in passing, that the settlers who, in their rage, demanded reprisals forgot just how disastrous their civilization had been to the native dwellers: for example, of the three to seven thousand Aborigines estimated to be living in Tasmania in 1804, there were probably only three hundred left by 1830. To Clark Aborigines are still peripheral to the story of Australia's development, and their contribution slight, but at least some measure of sympathy and understanding is given to their plight.

Clearer thinking and a more honest approach to the pervasiveness of Australian racism came with the publication of A. T. Yarwood's *Asian Migration to Australia*, where the attitudes leading to the White Australia Policy, even where unpalatable, are nevertheless recorded with objectivity. He recalls[7] that, by 1895, all the Australian colonies leaned to the view that 'no commercial benefits that we can conceive would be commensurate with the evils that might come upon Australia from an unrestricted inflow of Asiatics' (as a newspaper editorial expressed it). The ideal of racial purity was so firmly established that Prime Minister Barton in 1901 declared that 'legislation against Asian migration could be regarded simply as a matter of course', while W. B. Sawer told the House of Representatives that there would be no member of Parliament who would dare express opposition to the concept of a white Australia. Yarwood points out that the idea of the innate superiority of the white races was immanent in 1901 and comments apologetically that now 'we experience some difficulty in viewing the attitude of early twentieth century Australians in the context of their times',[8] apparently forgetting that such views, although not so openly expressed, are still today very much part of our cultural heritage. The lie was given to the traditional Labor argument that exclusion of non-whites was purely on an economic basis as a possible depressant of wage standards by the utterance of J. C. Watson, Leader of the Labor Party: 'The more educated, the more cunning he [the Oriental] becomes, the more able, with his peculiar ideas of social and business morality, to cope with the people here.'

There is a wealth of such sentiments, including those with a sexual rather than an economic connotation, from which the historian could have chosen. Another Labor leader, William Lane, for example, remarked in 1892: 'I would rather see my daughter ... dead in her coffin than kissing one of them [black men] on the mouth or nursing a little coffee-coloured brat that she was mother to.' A bush song at the turn of the century (one of many that could be invoked in this context) implores both men and maids to eschew coloureds of all races:

> For this is our most sacred trust,
> That ye shall in the full maintain,
> Whether in simple love, or lust—
> Keep white the strain.

In prose and verse on countless occasions the sexual exploits of the Chinese were darkly hinted at in an unending 'lock up your daughters' theme.

In a later work Yarwood was to submit the merits of 'mutual enrichment' as against 'the friction of multi-racial societies', an argument which is still being constantly debated. The author's introduction ends on the optimistic note that there has been a 'growth of tolerance in Australia and an undermining of the myth of white superiority'.[9] As with Clark, an attitude of sweet reasonableness pervades the Yarwood volumes, but the reasonableness is directed more towards the racist (who, after all, had cause for his fears) than to his victims: since restriction of non-European immigration had prevented the growth of minorities 'whose presence might have led to recurring diplomatic crises'.[10]

Palfreeman's volume on the White Australia policy[11] concerns administration rather than rationale. He accepts as starting point that by 1901 the overwhelming majority of Australians wanted to exclude non-Europeans and that the exclusion had been so successful that, at the time of his writing (1967), 99·7 per cent of the population was of European race. In another publication Palfreeman unequivocally takes sides:

Whatever the undertones and overtones of racial prejudice, the protection of the community against the importation of cheap labour and of an unassimilable minority was morally justified. It must be remembered that the Chinese and Polynesian immigrants in the nineteenth century were unskilled labourers and were in fact, by Australian sociological standards, non-assimilable.[12]

(One wonders what this author's views would be on the influx of Turkish and southern European migrants in recent years, equally unskilled and equally 'unassimilable'?)

The latest volume concerning White Australia, by London, is a thoroughly documented attempt to explain the liberalization of immigration policy in 1966. He sees the 1901 Act as having been an 'inextricable interweaving of traditional fears and historical inertia'[13] and quotes as example a further statement at the time by J. C. Watson: 'The objection I have to mixing of coloured people with the white people of Australia ... lies in the main in the possibility and probability of racial contamination'; while another member of the 1901 Federal Parliament asked that the new nation retain 'the noble ideal of a White Australia – a snow-white Australia if you will. Let it be pure and spotless.' London draws the reader's attention to the policy's 'categorical grouping of diverse individuals on the basis of skin pigmentation' as pointing undeniably to an underlying racism. Of all the studies of White Australia to date, that of London is the readiest to face its obvious and inherent racialism. Possibly objectivity was made easier by the fact that the author is not an Australian!

The historian Russel Ward maintained that most Australians since 1939 have ceased to be racists since racism does not accord with the national ideal of brotherhood and equality and instanced as illustration the integration without social disturbance of so many non-British migrants since 1945.[14] But by 1971 a sojourn in England had brought Ward the realization that his disclaimer was not shared by the world at large, which was aware of Australian participation in a war with strong racist overtones (Vietnam), was notorious for its reluctance to admit non-Europeans and was one of the last surviving colonial powers. He still believes, however, that we are being misunderstood: 'Most Australians *today* do not harbour racist feelings ... Colombo Plan students are generally treated as brothers and friends . . . we are trying, belatedly, to atone for our ancestors' genocide of the first black Australians.'[15] But he does blame previous historians for covering up the nasty realities of our racist past and admits that 'lingering racist attitudes' are still extant.

Australian racism was to receive its most strident exposé in *A New Britannia*[16] in which Humphrey McQueen states unequivocally that racism is the 'linchpin' of Australian nationalism and that 'the tribunes of racism in Australia have largely come from the leaders of the Labor Party'. Later, McQueen was to comment that Australia, while protesting anti-Communist ideology, fear of economic competition and avoidance of internecine strife, had never ceased to be racist.[17]

Xenophobic outpourings in Australian literature and journalism were also given light of day in *A New Britannia* and since then the final melting of the mateship myth has come with *The Glorious Years of Australia Fair*,[18] largely illustrated from the Sydney *Bulletin*, the Bushman's Bible, from its beginning in 1880 up to 1920. This rumbustious, rowdy journal had its heydey at the time of the rise of nationalism, of unionism and of political Labor, a time of great strikes and application of the principle of unrelenting ostracism of the 'scab'. It has always been regarded as radical, nationalist, anti-monarchical, proletarian and progressive; which it was, on most occasions. It was also rabidly and consistently racist. An early manifesto declared that it stood for 'Australia for the Australians – the cheap Chinaman, the cheap nigger and the cheap European pauper to be absolutely excluded.' At the same time the *Northern Miner* was declaring:

The whites in northern Queensland are an average lot, they shoot the male blacks and carry off the gins, just as they did in Victoria and New South Wales. There is no occasion for any howling about the business . . . the aboriginals must go somehow – lead, rum, or otherwise. The nigger has to go.

The *Bulletin* had similar views, more philosophically expressed:

> In Queensland the blacks are killed by cruelty, here [in New South Wales] they are killed by kindness; in one place men are guilty of murder, in the other of mercy. Of course, it is better to be merciful, but the blacks die all the same.

By 1883 the *Bulletin* was of the opinion that the Aborigines were dying out and that this would satisfactorily answer the Aboriginal question, the implication being that the sooner the whole thing was forgotten the better.

At almost the same time as the publication of *The Glorious Years* came two trilogies which have proved to be the most important accounts of race relations yet to appear in Australia: C. D. Rowley's *Aboriginal Policy and Practice*[19] and *Racism: The Australian Experience*, edited by F. S. Stevens.[20]

Rowley, in a work notable for its compassion and insight, gives endless documentation of the inherent racism manifest in almost all Aboriginal–white relations. He makes it difficult for us ever again to believe the twin legends of heroic pioneers and an egalitarian society. The author apologizes for the repetitiveness of his tale as he takes us from one State to the next, chronicling the unequal clashes over land between black and white, the indifference, bordering on contempt, with which Aborigines were treated, the cruelty and degradation which were their unending lot. Ceaseless disregard; deprivation of liberty; massive institutionalization (as a cheap way of avoiding race friction in the towns); attitudes varying from the benevolently paternal to the crudely exploitative; all these have produced a withdrawal on the Aboriginal side, an opting out from the major society which has clearly spurned them.

The unique contribution of the *Racism* volumes is that they give evidence of the inherent racialism of Australian history and culture and proceed to discuss as an integrated whole its many facets, its multiple causation and the role that it serves. For the first time we are aware of strong links between attitudes to migrants and Aborigines; policies towards Niugini, the United Nations, and southern Africa.

It still remains for an Aboriginal historian to write of the one-sided warfare against his race with the combination of passion and careful scholarship which has been evinced by several American Indians including Vine Deloria's *We Died for Their Sins*, which tells of the massacres and injustices perpetrated on his people.

Even this brief outline of some of the Australian race relations literature of the last half-century indicates the very considerable changes of viewpoint which have taken place over that period. Reflecting the public attitudes of the time, earlier historians selected their evidence to avoid or minimize an unending reiteration of manifestly racist sentiments. Gradually, with a change of public viewpoint, a more objective treatment of historic documents revealed the ingrained racial superiority with which most white Australians are imbued and which is one of the most important facts of life (as will be seen) with which black Australians in the country towns and elsewhere have to contend today.

Notes

1. WILLARD, MYRA, *History of the White Australia Policy to 1920*, Melbourne, 1928, p. 36.
2. LYNG, J., *Non-Britishers in Australia*, Melbourne, 1927.
3. LYNG, J., op. cit., p. 200.
4. Some of the arguments that Lyng puts forward for increased non-British immigration into Australia are a little unorthodox: to defend herself against floods and fires, diseases and pests. For 'while in the cities there is no end to strikes for higher pay or for principles of little importance to anybody ... the fair land of Australia is being laid waste by noxious weeds.' (p. 217)
5. HASLUCK, P. M. C., *Black Australians: A Survey of Native Policy in Western Australia 1829–1897*, Melbourne, 1942.

6. CLARK, C. MANNING, *A Short History of Australia*, fifth edition, Sydney, 1963, p. 14.

7. YARWOOD, A. T., *Asian Migration to Australia: The Background to Exclusion 1896–1923*, Melbourne, 1964, p. 7.

8. Ibid., p. 23.

9. YARWOOD, A. T., *Attitudes to Non-European Immigration*, Melbourne, 1968, p. 6.

10. YARWOOD, A. T., *Asian Migration to Australia*, p. 83.

11. PALFREEMAN, A. C., *The Administration of the White Australia Policy*, Melbourne, 1967.

12. [PALFREEMAN, A. C.], *Current Affairs Bulletin*, vol. 34, July 1964, p. 56 (as quoted in YARWOOD, A. T., *Attitudes to Non-European Immigration*, p. 124).

13. LONDON, H. I., *Non-White Immigration and the 'White Australia' Policy*, Sydney, 1970, p. 6.

14. WARD, RUSSEL, *The Australian Legend*, Melbourne, 1958.

15. WARD, RUSSEL, 'Home Thoughts from Abroad: Australia's Racist Image', *Meanjin Quarterly*, vol. 30, no. 2, pp. 149–56.

16. MCQUEEN, HUMPHREY, *A New Britannia*, Melbourne. 1970.

17. MCQUEEN, HUMPHREY, 'The Sustenance of Silence: Racism in Twentieth Century Australia', *Meanjin Quarterly*, vol. 30, no. 2, pp. 157–64.

18. INSON, GRAEME and WARD, RUSSEL, *The Glorious Years of Australia Fair from the Birth of the Bulletin to Versailles*, Melbourne, 1971.

19. ROWLEY, C. D., *Aboriginal Policy and Practice*, vol. 1, *The Destruction of Aboriginal Society*, Canberra, 1970; vol. 2, *Outcasts in White Australia*, Canberra, 1971; vol. 3, *The Remote Aborigines*, Canberra, 1971.

20. STEVENS, FRANK S. (ed.), *Racism: The Australian Experience*, vol. 1, *Prejudice and Xenophobia*, Sydney, 1971; vol. 2, *Black Versus White*, Sydney, 1972; vol. 3, *Colonialism*, Sydney, 1972.

Chapter Four

Public, Media and Pressure Groups

The historians can at least comfort themselves with the thought that they have reflected the opinion of their times, even, be it said, the relatively more enlightened section of that opinion. Surveys between 1947 and 1971 indicate a progressive softening of attitude towards the admission of non-Europeans as migrants, though this has not always proved to be a straight-out 'colour' question, being sometimes imbued with political considerations. Oeser and Hammond[1] report that their (Melbourne) respondents in 1947 feared that non-Europeans would not 'fit in', were not 'like us' or would become a threat to the Australian standard of living. Attitudes to Chinese were the least unfavourable of the three 'coloured' groups since as immigrants they were the most familiar and, as far as the Melbourne Chinese community was concerned, had integrated easily.

1947

	Keep out	Let a few in	Allow them to come	Try to get them to come
U.K.[2]	0·9	1·8	25	72
Chinese	26	42	23	8
Negro	68	23	9	0

By 1964 Huck[3] found that attitudes towards the Chinese had shifted, and they had become less acceptable. Australians were still willing to accept Chinese from Hong Kong and Singapore as being English-speaking and British-oriented, but unwilling to do so from mainland China, for fear of communist taint.

1964

	Keep out	Let a few in	Allow them to come	Try to get them to come
U.K.	2	6	37	54
Chinese	33	50	15	2
Negro	47	36	14	3

A 1971 *Age* poll[4] separated 'mainland' from 'other' Chinese and showed clearly that an unfavourable press had transferred to China the formerly Japanese role of 'Yellow Peril'.

1971

	Keep out	Let a few in	Allow them to come	Try to get them to come
English	3	17	60	19
Mainland Chinese	41	32	21	2
Other Chinese	19	43	33	3
Negro	34	32	29	3
Japanese	25	40	30	3

Despite the fact that attitudes to English and other European migrants had become less enthusiastic by this time – the overall immigration policy was being criticized as too ambitious and too great a strain on national resources – attitudes to non-Europeans had nevertheless become more favourable. The same views were being expressed in the Gallup polls,[5] which, from 1954 onwards, showed a steady increase in acceptance of non-Europeans as migrants. Governmental sensitivity to this change was to be, promptly if cautiously, translated into action. A relaxation of the restriction on Asian immigration in 1966 resulted in an increase of from 3,000 non-Europeans entering Australia as permanent settlers in that year to 9,000 in 1969.

The mass media have also changed their stance radically. In the last century the *Illustrated Sydney News* was declaiming on 21 December 1878:

We cannot get over our repugnance to the [Chinese] race whose tawny, parchment-coloured skins, black hair, lank and coarse, no beards, oblique eyes and high cheek bones distinguish them so widely from ourselves and place them so far beneath our recognized standards of manliness and beauty.

The *Commonweal*, dealing with a report to the Melbourne Trades Hall in 1892, commented:

One woman related how her daughter, fourteen years of age, had answered an advertisement for a nursegirl, the occupants of the house in Fitzroy to whom she applied being Chinese. Now, surely the police can take cognizance of this statement and prevent the defilement of the young girls of our community by the almond-eyed procurer or his leprous associates.

It is inconceivable that any Australian newspaper would have written in such naïve, yet vicious, strain during the last few decades, where cautious support has been given by at least a section of the press to a small increase in non-European immigraiton.

At the time that such blasts were being delivered against 'the Mongol' and 'the yellow Chinese', newspaper editorials were urging settlers to protect themselves from Aborigines by shooting them dead, since they were 'very low in moral condition and intellectual power'[6] and thus deserving of the harsh treatment consistently meted out to them. Such views have long since ceased to see the light of day and the tone of the media at the present time is favourable to Aborigines, if in a paternalistic way.

During the last decade scarcely a day has passed without some item of Aboriginal news in the press of the capital cities. These have tended to be of a personalized and mildly sensational kind, lacking carefully documented background information. (The same generalization is by and large true of items on the internal Australian scene not concerning race.) Quite recently there has been an increase in the level of information and understanding of the Aboriginal situation, but the 'cocooning' of the public with which the media in Australia have been justly accused usually comes into play, preventing the full exposition of social evils which are too unpleasant and too accusatory for the majority to face comfortably. An obvious area of inadequacy, where a whole Aboriginal community lives on a rubbish tip or where Aboriginal children die from malnutrition will be reported, but there is no ardent follow-up campaign which seeks change, no harrassment of politicians. A shocked editorial or two and an admonitory telecast will readily be quelled by the offer of a few more water-taps by the local authority or of a tour of inspection by a Cabinet minister.

Innumerable examples of this treatment could be cited. In January 1971 newspapers reported that twenty Aboriginal children, part of a fringe-dwelling community living on a reserve outside Wyndham, Western Australia, regularly raided garbage bins and caravans in a public park in search of food. The reserve 'housing' from which they came comprised tin, corrugated iron and concrete houses and run-down shacks. A report from the Wyndham Shire Council stated that 'the underlying cause of these raids can simply be stated as hunger'. The shire clerk proposed putting a high fence round the park from which the food had been taken. 'The Council had recently spent $74,000 on improvements, and did not want Aborigines running through it.'[7] The Minister for Native Welfare declared that the children were not hungry, but the then Director of the Aborigines Advancement League of Victoria (Mr B. McGuinness) squarely laid the blame for the food-stealing on the Western Australian Government.[8] After a few days of publicity the matter was dropped by the media and no information was forthcoming as to how this deplorable state of affairs had come to pass, whether it was widespread and if anything had been done to relieve the situation.

A few months previously (November 1970) there had been reports of a group of fifty Aborigines from the Northern Territory who were camped on the outskirts of Camoo-

43

weal in northern Queensland without water, garbage disposal, sanitation or shelter. Seven babies died of malnutrition or infection in six months. Angry talk among the whites of Camooweal centred on the health risk to the town which was threatened by the Aborigines' presence. Again just a bare report without detailed information, and no follow-up as to what, if anything, ensued. Presumably the public did not want to know whether any more babies died and how the situation could be prevented from recurring.

Attempts by Aborigines to become political activists and to press their claims more insistently are treated sensationally, with a scarcely concealed rubbing of hopeful hands at the possibility of violence (since this makes news), which is overtly deplored. Whether the recently formed Black Panther Party possesses or does not possess guns, and whether it proposes to use them, has received more attention than the very real grievances and positive programmes for self-education and change with which the party is sincerely concerned. And so, although Aboriginal items continue to feature daily in the media, the level of public information remains low.

Better-documented in their information and more formative in the slow and painful reappraisal of the role of the non-European have been the anti-racist pressure groups. Immigration Reform Groups sprang up in 1962 with the aim of having non-European migration accepted on the same basis as European, with 'our capacity to absorb migrants without social or economic strain as the sole determinant of level of intake'[9] and their publications aroused considerable discussion. The Australian Council of Churches advocated a system which would 'affirm our conviction of racial equality and remove suspicion that we are governed by colour prejudice'. The Australian Catholic bishops condemned the 'false assumption of racial superiority which too often underlies the White Australia policy'. On the other hand a leader of the Returned Services League in November 1961 saw the opponents of the policy 'as an unholy alliance of do-gooders, some influenced by communist organisations and others by religious bodies'; while the then New South Wales president of the same organization, Sir William Yeo, achieved enduring fame a few years later when at an RSL conference he expressed the opinion that all foreigners, and particularly those of eastern or Middle eastern extraction, were 'wogs, dogs, bogs or logs'.

Student demonstrations against apartheid took place in Sydney in March 1960 and against White Australia at the 1961 elections; there were Freedom Rides in northern New South Wales in 1965 to enforce Aboriginal entry to public places, while the many public demonstrations against the visiting South African Rugby team in 1971 determined the cancellation of the Springbok cricket tour, scheduled for later in that year. The demonstrations attracted large numbers of people who showed their strong feeling against racism in South Africa in no uncertain fashion. Aboriginal reaction to all the turmoil was inclined to be cynical. Why all the fuss, they asked, about the black people of another country, when so much injustice and suffering are allowed to continue in our own? The students took the point and formed the Anti-Racist Movement which would campaign in favour of Aborigines, Niuginians and non-European immigration, as well as against the apartheid of South Africa.

The churches have also taken up the cudgels on the Aboriginal behalf on the question of Land Rights (or the rights of Aboriginal groups to ownership of their traditional territories) and have tried to implement policies on church missions of more consultation and less control. Many church members have in recent years looked critically at mission policy and regretted the degree of control which white churchmen have had over Aborigines in strictly economic and practical areas for which their theological training had not equipped them. A group of clergymen have been instrumental in calling for more enlightened administration in Central Australia, where Aboriginal social disorientation, epitomized in an excessively high infant mortality rate, has spread alarmingly. Their statement in April 1972 included the words: 'We firmly believe that the

45

philosophy and practice of the Welfare Division of the Northern Territory administration is contributing markedly to the destruction of Aboriginal initiative and hopes of responsible advancement.'[10]

Nor is it only a handful of radical clergymen who are so forthright. Influential religious leaders have been equally outspoken. The Primate of the Anglican Church and the Anglican synod of the Canberra and Goulburn diocese have accused Australia of the unchristian act of racism;[11] and were joined by the Roman Catholic Archbishop of Sydney, who questioned the existence of racial tolerance in Australia.[12]

The trade union movement has, on the whole, been half-hearted in its anti-racist stance. The traditional unionist view of 'they'll take our jobs and lower our standard of living' dies hard. Yet, in September 1963, the Congress of the Australian Council of Trade Unions unanimously adopted a policy statement on Aborigines which included the words:

Congress declares that it is the natural right of the Aboriginal people to enjoy a social and legal equality with other Australians. Aboriginal people, while forming a part of the Australian population, are at the same time distinct, viable, national minorities entitled to special facilities for self-improvement.

Individual unions have been represented on Aboriginal civil rights organizations and have joined with students to support Aboriginal direct action, particularly with regard to the Gurindji people of the Northern Territory in their claims from 1967 onwards to occupancy of a portion of their tribal land.

Less publicized, but none the less effective, has been interest in Aboriginal affairs by a variety of professional groups who do not normally regard themselves as political lobbyists for matters outside their own discipline. The *Medical Journal of Australia* over the past decade has published a steady spate of articles concerned with the very high morbidity and mortality rates of Aboriginal communities. These have been concerned not alone with the medical facts of the situation but with the aetiology of diseases prevalent in government settlements in the Northern Territory: wretched 'housing', malnutrition, squalor and overcrowding, which make the task of prevention well-nigh impossible for the medical personnel concerned.

Architects have also acknowledged the cultural differences of Aborigines, particularly of those groups whose ways are still semi-tribal. Conferences have been arranged within the profession (sometimes with governmental assistance) to discuss plans for the type of housing which conforms to the expressed wishes of Aboriginal families who, while requiring adequate protection from the elements, may still want to be part of the community about them and not be completely enclosed. Such housing, too, must allow for large families and frequent visitors. The legal fraternity has assisted by forming Legal Aid services by which lawyers advise and defend Aborigines and are often able to bring about changes in administration and police procedures by their very presence.

Members of the teaching profession have also shown increasing concern with Aboriginal affairs, conducting surveys of their educational position and providing seminars on the teaching of Aborigines (recognizing that they are both culturally different and disadvantaged as a group) and on teaching about Aborigines and other ethnic groups in such a way as to increase tolerance. Several Federal parliamentarians in both the House and Senate, after travelling widely in Aboriginal areas and listening to Aboriginal grievances, have formed themselves into effective lobbyists, hammering the government to effect improvements.

The early 1960s saw the formation of two organizations specifically to promote Aboriginal research: the Australian Institute for Aboriginal Studies in Canberra, funded by the Commonwealth government; and the Centre for Research into Aboriginal Affairs, Melbourne, largely financed by Monash University. By this time the field of Aboriginal studies, long the province of the anthropologists, was being investigated by academics of many disciplines and their work was now supported and publicized by these and other semi-official bodies.

Scientific information on Aborigines has also been disseminated by a number of Aboriginal civil rights groups which since the late 1950s have grown up in all parts of Australia. These have been co-ordinated under the Federal Council for the Advancement of Aborigines and Torres Strait Islanders (FCAATSI) which has welcomed to its ranks representatives of the Employers' Federation and the Unions, the churches, members of all political parties, service groups and private citizens. FCAATSI was influential in obtaining the 1967 referendum which led to Commonwealth participation in Aboriginal affairs and has crusaded for many years for Land Rights. Apart from disseminating scientific knowledge of Aborigines it has also publicized the position of ethnic minorities in other lands. Although the Aboriginal 'advancement' organizations (as they were at first called), were originally white-dominated, their control has been taken into Aboriginal hands in the last few years and they have become less patient and more militant: one of the demands of the all-Aboriginal section of the 1972 annual conference of FCAATSI was for the resignation of the Director of Social Welfare for the Northern Territory on the basis of his 'persistent lack of effective action to come to grips with increasingly urgent Aboriginal problems.' Some of the younger urban Aborigines have now formed various Black Action groups who are demanding more Aboriginal power in the form of funds and technical assistance, so that they can manage their own affairs independent of white control.

The government cannot altogether ignore this barrage of protests, and has been forced to concede a number of points. Land rights have not been accorded, but a fund has been set up for the leasing and development of land by Aboriginal individuals and groups. The promise of cessation of discriminatory legislation by the end of 1972 does not look as though it will be fulfilled, but at least Queensland has amended its legislation and eliminated the control of the finances of its reserve dwellers. The infant mortality rate of Central Australia continues to be appallingly high, but a sop was given to public discontent by the acquisition of additional hospital accommodation. The former official policy of assimilation or racial suicide was changed to integration, and some lip-service at least is paid to the value of the Aboriginal traditional culture (though it is likely that, in practice, 'culture' often stands for arts and artefacts rather than the whole way of life of a people). The Prime Minister (Mr W. McMahon), in his statement to the Conference of Ministers Responsible for Aboriginal Affairs in April 1971, declared:

We believe that Aboriginal Australians should be assisted as individuals and, if they wish, as groups to hold effective and respected places within one Australian society with equal access to the rights and opportunities it provides and accepting responsibilities towards it. At the same time they should be encouraged and assisted to preserve and develop their culture – their languages, traditions and arts – so that these can become living elements in the diverse culture of the Australian society.

One would like to add the rider: administrators, please note!

Public pressure against the White Australia policy has also been acknowledged by a series of governmental pronouncements, often obscure and self-contradictory. Said Mr Snedden, then Minister for Immigration, in 1968:

If we ask what gains there would be in setting out deliberately to create a multi-racial society, there seems no case for substantial changes in Australia's existing policies. Australia's aim is to maintain a predominantly homogeneous population.[13]

The following year he was to express this viewpoint more strongly.

If [Asian] migration implied multi-cultural activities within Australian society, then it is not the type Australia wants. We must be a single Australian people and that's a view I strongly hold.[14]

He was to be contradicted – or seemingly so – by his Prime Minister (John Gorton) in Singapore a short time later, when the latter, no doubt carried away on wings of oratory before a mostly Asian audience, proclaimed that 'Australia may provide the first truly multi-racial society with no tensions of any kind'. In answer to questioning he backed down a little, stating that it was an expression of an ideal, the reality being that 'we must remain homogeneous . . . People of other races can come in and be assimilated'.[15]

It was in Singapore also that Gorton, in his address to this same audience, included the words:

I don't think those of you who have been there [in Australia] will have noticed any racism unless you were extraordinarily unfortunate while you were living in my country. There is legal discrimination still in some Australian States against Aboriginals . . . I think there are other countries where racial discrimination may be more pronounced than it is in my own.[16]

This is an example of the muddle-headedness for which the former Prime Minister was famed. What he is saying in effect, as chief government spokesman in an allied country, is 'The racism we have is not against actual people and anyway, it could be a whole lot worse.' That this *was*, in fact, his line of thinking was proved at a subsequent tele-vision conference when, in describing the present hetero-geneity of the Australian population, he said, 'We have Australians, we have Aboriginals, we have Australians of Chinese extraction, of Japanese extraction.'[17] The juxtapositon of Australians *and* Aborigines is one that is frequently made, and not just by politicians.

Shortly afterwards Minister for Immigration A. J. Forbes was to express hurt that a Labor politician had referred to 'racial bigots in the corridors of power' and to 'a stance of ethnic superiority', when all the government wanted by its rectriction of non-Europeans was to avoid trouble.[18] According to these spokesmen the propensity for trouble-making on the part of people with coloured skins is endlessly high, their powers of integration just as endlessly low.

Government denials have had no effect on the spate of criticism of Australia's race policies which has continued and grown in recent years both abroad and at home. Among visiting social scientists has been a young American political observer who, after four years' sojourn in Canberra, let off a departing blast: 'Deep-seated racism ... is manifested in the restrictive immigration policy ... The majority of Australians can easily live their entire lives without ever meeting a non-white face-to-face, and can thus continue to nurture their racial supremacy ignorance.'[19]

A visiting Canadian psychologist was even more vehement, describing White Australia as 'one of the more flagrant examples of racism in the world'. Intolerance was also reflected in the wanton neglect of Aborigines and the demand for total assimilation of migrants 'with a complete disregard for the enrichment the culture of the various minority groups could bring'.[20] (This latter reference was to the action of the Marrickville RSL in demanding that migrants speak English at their club.)

Another visiting post-graduate researcher to enter the fray was Allan Healy, who had been studying Australian administration in New Guinea against his own background of experience in several non-Western cultures in Africa.

What surprises me is that anyone feels it necessary to *argue* that Australians are racists. It is so patent that argument is superfluous. Admittedly the policy to keep the Volk pure has

51

produced a society where the opportunities for explicit racist expression are limited. Among intellectuals, it generally takes the form of poorly disguised inter-cultural contempt ... anyone who seriously advocates the study of Africa is considered moonstruck.[21]

A determined patriot might say, with some justification, that the mere fact that such vehement criticism is published is an indication of feelings of guilt and a desire for their expiation.

The mood of the electorate is still ambivalent on the question of racial minorities in our midst and this ambivalence finds its reflection in the current immigration policy of the Australian Labor party, the basis of which is, *inter alia*:

The avoidance of the difficult social and economic problems which may follow from an influx of peoples having different standards of living, traditions and cultures.
The avoidance of discrimination on any grounds of race or colour of skin or nationality.[22]

In the ensuing Senate debate, Labor spokesmen proclaimed that educated Asians or Papuans with required skills would obtain assisted passages under this policy, which were not available under the present government. On the other hand, first preference would go to migrants nominated by Australians, so that in fact fewer Asian migrants would be entering than at present. A neat tactic whereby both anti-racist and racist critics are subdued at one blow.

The even tenor of Australia's political life was stirred in the period shortly before the election campaign of 1972 by a sudden flare-up of racial views, which indicated that White Australia continues to be a live and highly emotive issue and that the line-up of pro- and anti-racist forces is not necessarily on Party lines.

A Cabinet Minister (Mr Donald Chipp) made the comment (1 May 1972) that he would like to see Australia be-

come a multi-racial society in the 1980s. (It is noteworthy
that even a person of such liberal outlook forgets that
multi-racialism in this country dates back to 1788.) The
former leader of the Labor Party (Mr Arthur Calwell)
countered by stating that the 'flood of coloured migrants'
who had been 'pouring into Australia' 'lived on the smell
of an oily rag and bred like flies', thus lowering community
living standards and leading to a 'chocolate-coloured Australia' a state of affairs which any 'red-blooded Australian'
would deplore.[23] Labor politicians, both Federal and State,
promptly charged to the side of their political opponent,
Mr Chipp; if any agreed with Calwell, they kept a prudent
silence. The Minister for Immigration (Dr Forbes) reiterated the well-worn Liberal party policy of a 'predominantly
homogenous society' which Chipp maintained was what he
had meant all along. Most television channels gave more
time to Chipp supporters than to those of Calwell. The
press were more divided, many newspapers being careful
not to alienate their racist readers too much, though without wanting to appear racist themselves. The Adelaide
Advertiser cautiously praised Chipp but ignored Calwell,
who nevertheless earned the enthusiastic support of the
Sydney *Daily Telegraph*. The *Daily Mirror* of Sydney and
the *Age* and *Herald* of Melbourne wholeheartedly deplored
his viewpoint. The *Australian*, while finding the phraseology
tasteless, approved Calwell's sentiments; the *Canberra
Times* regretted them. A variety of voluntary organizations
came forth with anti-racist statements and it seemed likely
that both the major political parties would find it expedi-
ent not to highlight policies concerning immigration of non-
Europeans in their election campaigns, particularly after an
Australia-wide Gallup Poll (July 1972) showed that 49 per
cent of those questioned disapproved Chipp's policy for a
multi-racial society, 37 per cent approved and 14 per cent
were undecided.

Notes

1. OESER, O. A. and HAMMOND, S. B., *Social Structure and Personality in a City*, London, 1954, p. 64.
2. U.K. citizens have consistently been the most favoured of all migrants and are therefore included for purposes of comparison.
3. HUCK, ARTHUR, *Australian Attitudes to the Chinese*, Melbourne, 1964, p. 7.
4. *Age* Poll, reported in the *Age* (Melbourne), 19 July 1971.
5. For details, see LONDON, H. I., *Non-White Immigration and the 'White Australia' Policy*, Sydney, 1970, p. 151. For public opinion relating to attitudes towards Aborigines, see Chapters 7 and 12.
6. *Argus* (Melbourne), July 1861, as quoted in HALL, R. V., 'Racism and the Press', in STEVENS, F. S. (ed.), *Racism: The Australian Experience*, vol. 1, Sydney, 1971, which gives an account of the early racial attitudes of the Australian press.
7. *Age*, 13 January 1971.
8. *Australian*, 14 January 1971.
9. RIVETT, K. (ed.), *Immigration: Control or Colour Bar?*, Melbourne, 1962, p. 135.
10. *Age*, 3 April 1972.
11. *Age*, 5 August 1971.
12. FREEMAN, ARCHBISHOP, *Australian*, 31 August 1971.
13. SNEDDEN, B. M., *Looking at Some Aspects of Australia's Immigration Policy*, Government Printer, Canberra, 1968, p. 9.
14. *Australian*, 26 July 1969.
15. Interview given by the Prime Minister, Mr John Gorton, for ABC Television, 25 January 1971, official transcript, p. 8.
16. Speech by the Prime Minister at the Australian Alumni Dinner in Singapore, 18 January 1971, official transcript, p. 6.
17. Interview given by Prime Minister, op. cit., p. 9.
18. News release from the Minister for Immigration, Canberra, 21 July 1971.
19. KAHAN, MICHAEL, *Australian*, 18 January 1971.
20. BERRY, J. W., *Age*, 9 May 1969.

21. HEALY, ALLAN, 'The Intercultural Problem: Isolated Australians', *Meanjin Quarterly*, January 1970, pp. 57–63.
22. Commonwealth of Australia, *Parliamentary Debates* (Hansard), Senate no. 23, 2 December 1971, p. 235.
23. *Herald* (Melbourne), 2 May 1971. One is reminded of Professor W. E. H. Stanner's definition of a racist as one who displays 'a splendid credulity towards the unlikely and an iron resolve to believe the improbable.' (The Boyer Lectures 1968, *After the Dreaming*, Australian Broadcasting Commission, p. 30.)

Chapter Five

Racism and the Extreme Right

The anti-racist groups have been unco-ordinated, desultory and pragmatic; often stronger in ideals than in organization. Many of them have sprung into existence for a specific purpose, be it the preparation of a conference or the promotion of better Aboriginal living conditions in a particular area. But all have been open and straightforward, operating under clearly stated aims and methods and allowing politicians and administrators under attack publicly to deny or defend their actions.

The activities of the Extreme Right, those groups who form the ultra-conservative edge of the political spectrum, have been more clandestine and more insidious, frequently lending covert support to each other. They have tended to form a variety of sub-groups whose names are deliberately chosen to suggest democracy and fraternity, but whose aim is reactionary and racist. During the previously mentioned anti-apartheid demonstrations of 1971 students, trades unionists and others were to discover that these groups had more hitting power (in an all too literal sense) than had previously been attributed to them. In fact it was now truer to say that they had become of the extrem*ist* Right, since their violent tactics placed them outside the institutional structure of society.[1] Their anti-communism, anti-socialism, racism, intense nationalism and militarism and their espousal of racist régimes have found support at least in some aspects from various government Members, both in the State and Federal Houses, who grace their public platforms from time to time, thus lending an aura of respectability and helping to increase attendances.

Professor Stanner commented recently that 'we have few if any organizations making it their business to build or nurture an extreme ideology of hate'.[2] The evidence is that there are a number of small but vociferous organizations whose main aim *is* to stir up hate, and that their membership is growing.[3] They thrive on publicity, even that of a seemingly adverse kind. The Director of the Australian League of Rights, Eric Butler, frequently gloats in one or other of his publications on the amount of public attention which the League is receiving; *Voices of Hate*, which its author, Kenneth Gott, intended as an anti-Right polemic has to a certain extent rebounded and is sold at League meetings; and, after a public affairs programme on Australian Broadcasting Commission television on the Australian Nazi Party which stressed its extreme intolerance, illogicality and authoritarianism, membership of the Party actually increased.

1960 saw the formation of the Australian Christian Anti-Communist Crusade which was joined on the extreme Right in 1961 by the Defend Australia League and a variety of migrant organizations, including the Hungarista Movement which shares platforms with the Nazis. The credo of the radical Right migrants is anti-socialism, anti-Russianism and anti-Semitism. In 1965 there was formed in Brisbane Citizens for Freedom, whose president, Harold Wright, was to object to the support of an Aboriginal protest demonstration by the Australian Council of Churches;[4] and at about the same time the Immigration Control Association, to prevent non-European immigration.

1961 saw, too, the embryo of the Nazi Party with the formation of the Australian Workers' Nationalist Party, which was to change its name in each successive year (Australian National Socialist Movement in 1962, Australian National Renascent Party in 1963, Australian National Centre Party in 1964) until it emerged in 1965 as the full-formed National Socialist Party of Australia, which commemorates the birthday of 'our founder, Adolf Hitler', is anti-socialist, pro-Vietnam war, and has as its chief aim the 'protection of Western civilization' which, of course, automatically excludes Jews and blacks. Intending members must sign an avowal: 'I am of Aryan stock', though how the applicant can guarantee this is not made clear. The policy of the party on Aborigines is based on the apartheid of South Africa: separation without consultation. The Federal secretary, Mrs Katrina Young, recently stated that Aborigines should have a 'second State'.[5] At a student meeting, her husband had confirmed that the Party, when in power, would set aside a tract of land (whereabouts unknown) for Aborigines, the direction of which would be progressively transferred to Aborigines as they acquired the necessary training and sufficient numbers. A 'Morals Act' would prevent Aborigines marrying whites, and the immigration of coloured people would be banned 'otherwise the whole place would turn into a black man's ghetto'.[6]

The chief Nazi publication is the *Australian National Socialist Journal*, a quarterly founded in 1968 which has as its slogan, 'For Race and Nation'. 'Race is the hub or nucleus of National Socialist philosophy; around it all other considerations revolve.'[7]

The *Journal* has claimed Henry Lawson as one of its own and cites impressive evidence in support, including:

> I see the brown and yellow rule
> O'er southern land and southern waves,
> White children in the heathen school,
> And black and white together slaves;
> I see the colour-line so drawn
> (I see it plain and speak I must)
> That our brown masters of the dawn
> Might, aye, have fair girls for their lusts![8]

Details of members' corporate activities are given State by State in the *National Socialist Bulletin*. The Victorian branch had a busy month in July 1971 when Comrades 'took action to disrupt the Moratorium and the peace-creeps'; went to Olympic Park to welcome the Springbok rugby players, managing to tear down more than a dozen anti-apartheid banners; and attended on 4 July an anti-American demonstration, only to discover that their presence was not required since 'the police handled the demonstrators superbly'. In 1970 Cawthron, then national secretary of the Nazi Party, stood for the Canberra by-election (the first time a Nazi candidate had presented) and polled 175 votes. In the Senate elections of that year Nazi candidates stood in Victoria, New South Wales and Queensland. The highest percentage of Nazi votes in any one State was gained by the Queenslander, K. W. D. Thompson: 1·5 per cent (his name appeared first on the ballot paper, so it can fairly be assumed that a certain proportion were 'donkey votes' of people who number candidates in order down the list). The Nazis polled a total of 22,000 votes for the three States.

By far the strongest of the parties of the extreme Right is the Australian League of Rights, which must have considerable funds at its disposal, judging by the number of its activities, publications and paid organizers. The League is a descendent of the Social Credit movement of the 1930s, centred on the writings of the late C. H. Douglas, originally a major in the British Army and later to live in Canada. His economic theories, based on the creation by government of extra money as a cure for economic ills, has been discredited by all reputable economists. Both the League's weekly journal, *On Target*, and the monthly *New Times* are consistently racist and its race 'expert' has maintained that in 'lower types' (that is non-whites and Jews) reason is subordinated to prejudice; therefore such people cannot be trusted with basic human rights, otherwise they will set up a racial supremacy leading to anti-white aggression.[10]

Affiliates of the League of Rights include the Institute of Economic Democracy, founded in 1969, which presents a quarterly journal, *Enterprise*, principally concerned with rural industries; the women's LILAC League (Ladies in Line against Communism) with its fortnightly *Ladies Line*; and the Christian Institute for Individual Freedom, whose prayer letter and information bulletins appear at frequent intervals; while the associated Heritage bookshop in Melbourne sells Right-wing publications, both local and imported, many of them of a blatantly anti-Semitic character. Recently the League held a seminar at which the Australian Heritage Society was formed. On this occasion a former professor of tropical medicine from Queensland, Sir Raphael Cilento, suggested that 'migrants should be examined for disease and purity of blood, the same as cattle imported into Australia'. At the same time the League's Director, Eric Butler, maintained that the Church's sole aim was 'to join with revolutionaries to stop people watching the type of sport they want to watch and to give money to the savages in Africa armed by communists.'[11]

From October 1970 onwards the League worked very hard, infiltrating the depressed rural areas, particularly in northern New South Wales and Queensland, imbuing dispirited farmers and graziers with their ideas on the causes and solutions of the rural crisis. The Institute of Economic Democracy holds seminars to demonstrate that rural depression is an international Jewish-Zionist-Socialist conspiracy, solvable by huge continuing loans at low or no interest. When Eric Butler debated the issue with Queensland Country Party politicians at Dalby R.S.L. hall near Toowoomba, on 4 November 1970, it was to a packed audience of seven hundred people.

Membership of the League usually involves participation in one of the well over a hundred Voters' Policy Associations or League branches which exist in urban and rural areas in all States. These were begun in 1964 as the 'actionist' arm of the League and have rapidly increased in number, especially in Victoria and Queensland. Members are required to take part in persistent letter writing to members of parliament and to newspapers, pursuing eternal vigilance in the 'battle for civilization' against an equally eternal international Jewish-socialist conspiracy to let loose the forces of barbarism in the form of a World State. Apart from these highly organized letter-writing campaigns against set targets (be they anti-apartheid demonstrators or the president of the Australian Council of Trade Unions), there is specific activity on the part of Electors' Associations to exert pressure on sitting members of parliament or on candidates. Early in 1971 the first such association was formed in Victoria, in the Murray electorate, where the three candidates at a by-election were invited to attend a meeting to answer questions. Only the Labor Party candidate declined to attend or to declare his opposition to 'any change in our traditional immigration policy'. The fact that the other candidates complied is an indication of the seriousness with which League influence is regarded by active politicians, and of the aura of respectability it has achieved. Since that time over thirty further Electors' Associations have been formed as 'non-party, non-power-seeking groups designed to rekindle individual initiative and responsibility in politics'. In the regular supplement to *On Target*, a bulletin for members only, dated 30 April 1971 their aim was stated more accurately and more bluntly as having the purpose of educating 'a wider section of the community in League aims and objectives, and thus bringing more of the right sort of pressure'. One could hardly disagree with Butler's statement (in *On Target* of 7 November 1971) that the associations had been one of the major achievements of the League over the preceding year and are 'a striking confirmation of the reality of League growth'. Further evidence of the League's political importance came with the statement in July 1971 of the Australian Labor Party's federal spokesman on industrial affairs (C. R. Cameron) that the League had infiltrated the Country Party and had actually been in control of the Party's conference at Lake Macquarie, New South Wales, in January 1971. He also asserted that nine or ten Federal politicians on the government side were influenced by the League. His statement received assent from the chairmen of the Queensland, New South Wales and Victorian Country Party, while Federal Country Party leader Anthony admitted that the League 'was trying to use the Country Party to push its own views'.[12]

Words or Blows

As early as December 1966 the League was claiming that 'in a sizeable number of electorates, excellent relationships have been established with members [of Parliament]' and by 28 April 1967 the bulletin to *On Target* reported in triumph that League groups in Victoria and South Australia had been 'playing a leading role in the election of office-bearers in both the Country Party and the Liberal Party'. One typically successful manoeuvre was the recent action of the Yarra North branch of the Liberal Party which, under the influence of a League president and other League members, demanded a government investigation into Black Power in Australia.[13]

Notes

1. The authors of *The Politics of the Extreme Right*, Sydney, 1967, R. W. CONNELL and FLORENCE GOULD, had maintained at the time of their writing that there was no extremist Right in Australia. We move on ...

2. STANNER, W. E. H., 'Introduction: Australia and Racialism', in *Prejudice and Xenophobia*, vol. 1 of STEVENS, F. S. (ed.), *Racism: The Australian Experience*, Sydney, 1971, p. 13.

3. In addition to CONNELL and GOULD, op. cit., see GOTT, K. D., *Voices of Hate*, Melbourne 1965; LEIBLER, I., 'Australia's Radical Right', *Quadrant*, March–April 1966, pp. 15–19 and a series of articles on the League of Rights by RICHARDSON, MICHAEL in the *Age* and *Sydney Morning Herald*, 26, 28, 29 February, 1 March 1972.

4. Letter to the *Age*, 18 December 1971.

5. *Sydney Sun*, 1 April 1971.

6. *Lot's Wife* (Melbourne), 21 July 1970.

7. *National Socialist Bulletin*, no. 20, July 1971, p. 1.

8. WENBERG, E. R., 'Our National Socialist Folk Heritage: Henry Lawson', *Australian National Socialist Journal*, vol. 2, no. 1, pp. 3–6.

9. *National Socialist Bulletin*, op. cit., p. 1.

10. WATTS, D., 'Who are the Racist Fanatics?' *New Times*, vol. 37, no. 11, November 1971, p. 4; and 'The Assault

upon Rights and Freedom', *New Times*, vol. 37, no. 9, September 1971, pp. 4–6.

11. *Sun* (Melbourne), 20 September 1971.

12. *Sunday Australian*, 8 August 1971.

13. Statement by President, Yarra North branch, Liberal Party on ABC radio 3AR current affairs programme (A.M.), 25 February 1972. For further details of League influence on the government parties see RICHARDSON, M., *Age*, 29 February and 1 March 1972.

Chapter Six

Discrimination
National and International

Although it has officially condemned racism as such, the government has scarcely interfered with the activities of these and other groups of the Extreme Right and has permitted various of its members to continue in their support both at Federal and State level. Similarly, on the international scene, though lip-service is paid to anti-racist resolutions of the United Nations, in practice these are often thwarted. A case in point is the International Convention on the Elimination of all Forms of Racial Discrimination, passed by the General Assembly in December 1965 with the concurrence of Australia. The Federal government, however, did not approach the States until April 1967 concerning changes in State legislation deemed necessary to enable Australia to sign the convention. In March 1970 discussions on the subject took place with the States at the Standing Committee of Commonwealth and State Officers on Aboriginal Affairs and on 9 July 1971, Prime Minister McMahon, in reply to a letter from the Australian Committee to Combat Racism and Racial Discrimination stated that

It is not possible for me to indicate at this stage when Australia might become a party to the Convention .. It is not the practice of the Commonwealth to ratify a convention, unless it is quite sure that the law and practice of the Commonwealth and States satisfy the requirements of the convention ... With reference to discriminating legislation against Aborigines, the government has pledged that it will all be removed by the end of 1972.

The discriminatory legislation to which the Prime Minister referred related to Queensland and Western Australia and has in fact since been repealed. However, the new *Abo-*

rigines Act and the *Torres Strait Islanders Act* of Queensland still retain discriminatory features. There are special tests of eligibility for candidates standing for election to Reserve councils which differ from those of local authorities in the general community; and these councils consist of two elected and two appointed representatives with power of veto vested in the Director of Aboriginal and Island Affairs. Ownership of so-called Aboriginal and Island Reserves remains solely with the government and the Director can still exert a large measure of conrol over Aboriginal lives by granting or withholding special assistance, at his discretion.

In effect the 30,000 Aborigines and Torres Strait Islanders who live on the Queensland reserves and church missions feel themselves to be institutionalized to a high degree both by legislation and by administrative practice. Many adults are paid about half the basic wage, since they are designated as 'trainees'. Most are government employees, fearful of losing their jobs or dropping to the end of the housing queue if they fall out with the local (white) manager.

Some of the residents of Palm Island reserve recently complained that they had had to negotiate with the bureaucracy in Brisbane for two years to get a replacement for a fishing boat lost in a storm and on which their livelihood depended. When the boat was finally sent, it was inadequate for their purposes. In order to visit the mainland, these island residents have to avail themselves of a government-owned and operated boat, on which their passage can be prevented by the local manager. Their lives are controlled by white officials and they themselves are rendered powerless, all within the framework of the law.

Although the Prime Minister did not refer to it, there is also discriminatory (Federal) legislation in the Northern Territory, where access to reserves by non-Aborigines is at the discretion of the Director of Social Welfare or his officers, not of the Aborigines concerned; and where a welfare officer may suspend for up to thirty days the right of any person to enter and remain on a reserve. Such reserves are white-controlled institutions with responsibility for their management and for the education, housing, employment and health of their inmates vested in an all-powerful bureaucratic structure.

The General Assembly of the United Nations adopted two further conventions on human rights in December 1966: the International Covenant on Economic, Social and Cultural Rights and the International Covenant on Civil and Political Rights; and again Australia voted in favour of both. Once more the Commonwealth wrote to the States (in June 1967) concerning alterations to State legislation deemed necessary before ratification; but again no finality was reached. In May 1971 the Prahran (Victoria) Court of Petty Sessions was told that eviction proceedings were being taken against a tenant on the grounds that she was allowing a Kenyan nurse to stay with her.

Australia abstained from voting on two further conventions of the International Labour Organization concerned with race discrimination: Number 107, Indigenous and Tribal Populations, 1957 and Number 111, Discrimination (Employment and Occupation), 1958. The former requires that recognition be given to the right of ownership, collective or individual, of indigenous peoples over lands which they have traditionally occupied. Although the Commonwealth is obliged to have periodic consultations with the States to give effect to ILO conventions and consults each April at the meeting of the Department of Labour Advisory Committee, it would appear that it has had no consultations on the Indigenous and Tribal Populations Convention since 1960.

The Discrimination (Employment and Occupation) Convention requires the elimination of any discrimination on the basis of race, colour, sex, religion, political opinion, national extraction or social origin. There have been frequent consultations with the States on this convention, in 1960, 1964 and every year since 1966, but the Commonwealth has still not ratified it because only one State has so far signified its agreement.

Throughout the 1950s the Australian government opposed any United Nations resolutions condemning apartheid, on the grounds that this was a domestic issue which concerned South Africa alone. However, during Sir Robert Menzies' brief term as Minister for External Affairs in 1960–1 he wrote (in mid-1960) to Prime Minister Verwoerd of South Africa urging changes in some of South Africa's racial policies and to President Salazar of Portugal, requesting self-determination for Angola. (Neither admonishment had any effect.)

Australia supported resolutions condemning apartheid during the 1960s but, in November 1969, reverted to opposition of such a motion although it was supported by eighty-three members of the United Nations with twenty absentions. At the same session votes were recorded in the General Assembly on twelve resolutions from the Fourth Committee relating to Trust and non-self-governing territories. On all these controversial questions of colour and colonies Australia did not oppose South Africa and Portugal but consistently voted against all her neighbours in south-east Asia and in the Asian Commonwealth.

Tacit support for the white majority government of Rhodesia, too, has not been lacking. Certain officials of the Rhodesian government born in Australia and no longer granted British passports were able to move about freely in those countries which did not recognize the Rhodesian régime after the Unilateral Declaration of Independence because they were issued with Australian travel documents. The régime's Secretary of External Affairs was granted an Australian passport by the Australian Embassy in Pretoria in June 1967, while the Rhodesian diplomatic representatives in Portugal and South Africa received their respective Australian passports within the next year.* When it was disclosed, in April 1972, that the Rhodesia Information Centre in Sydney was illegally importing propaganda con-

* In July 1972, after considerable pressure from Ghana, the Australian government announced that these three passports would not be renewed after their expiry date.

cerning the Smith régime, the Prime Minister announced
that no action would be taken to close the Centre.

At the Commonwealth Heads of State Conference in
Singapore in January 1971 (at which Prime Minister Gorton had made his euphoric remarks concerning race relations in this country), Australia was alone in supporting
the Heath government of Great Britain in its willingness
to sell arms to South Africa.

The United Nations Security Council adopted man-
datory sanctions against the Smith régime of Rhodesia, on
the grounds of its illegality, in May 1968. In September of
that year, the Australian Minister for External Affairs sent
a message to the Secretary-General setting out Australia's
intention to comply. Clause 3D of the United Nations resolution had prohibited trade except in 'special humanitarian
circumstances'. This saving clause enabled Australia to
bend her undertaking and to increase exports to Rhodesia
in the ensuing two years, until now we have become the
second biggest supplier to that country. Exports to South
Africa have risen substantially over the last decade from
$14 million to $86 million. The ambivalence of attitude towards the racist régimes in southern Africa must be viewed
against the rising volume of trade between this area and
Australia.

It can be seen, then, that the main political parties who
formulate and administer public policies on race matters
must constantly walk a tight-rope in order to accommodate
the views of not only the majority of their constituents and
of the openly political pressure groups on all sides, but of
traders and trade unionists, importers and manufacturers;
all those whose livelihood is linked with the nation's economic and political concerns. Similarly, a host of factors
impinge indirectly on the opinions of our citizen of the
country towns. He will be influenced by the main findings
of the scientists concerning race, and the world-wide revul-
sion to racism marked by the excesses of Nazi Germany.
The mass media may not in themselves be a formative in-

fluence, but they will at the very least draw up the agenda of what is being publicly discussed, and at what length. In like subtle vein, the activities of the pressure groups will also filter through to him, acting on his sensibilities, feeding his prejudices or appealing to his humanity. The milieu in which he lives has undergone a transformation. The main reflectors of public opinion – the historians, the media and the polls – all indicate a general change from the intense xenophobia of the early days to a more egalitarian creed, yet to be translated into action.

These and a hundred other influences will be acting on our citizen of the country towns, pushing and pulling him in a variety of subtle ways, interacting on his individual personality and background. Small wonder that his views concerning race often appear confused and his attitudes self-contradictory.

Part Two

The Four Country Towns

Chapter Seven

The Survey

So far, we have been considering race relations in Australia macroscopically, encompassing the main influential factors of both past and present. In order to gain a 'total' picture of the situation, we need to look at small areas in some detail in order to study the interaction of black and white citizens in their daily lives; their mutual attitudes; and the socio-economic position which Aboriginal communites are likely to occupy.

With this end in view, a survey of race relations in four country towns was undertaken during 1969 and 1970 which, it was hoped, would lead to increased understanding and therefore amelioration of Aboriginal conditions.

Few, if any, such studies have previously been conducted, and it is significant that the earlier race-relations literature was concerned more with white than with Aboriginal attitudes. At the back of the researchers' minds had been the anxious thought: But are They conforming? And are They acceptable?

One of the earliest pieces of research along these lines, had been in 1955, 'The Acceptability of Aboriginal Children in Queensland'[1] which was followed by studies of the attitudes of whites towards Aborigines by various social scientists, the first of whom was Hugh Philp, who discovered that a quarter of his Australia-wide white sample had had no contact at all with Aborigines. His work was followed a decade later by surveys in selected areas of Western Australia and also in New South Wales.[2]

Public opinion polls conducted in 1954, 1961 and 1965 indicated generally favourable attitudes towards Aborigines, a small majority of Australians (except in South Australia and Western Australia) believing that Aborigines of the full descent should have the right to drink alcohol and to vote, and that more should be spent on their education and housing. These polls are not strictly comparable with those on attitudes to Asian migration (see Chapter 2) since the former were concerned with the desirability of admission of Asians, not of the treatment of those already living in Australia. A national referendum conducted in May 1967 gave a majority of 89 per cent to a proposition that Aborigines be included in the census and that the Federal government be given the power to legislate on their behalf. The result stemmed partly from a massive publicity campaign conducted by the Aboriginal civil rights movement, in particular by FCAATSI, and was only the fifth time in sixty-six years that the Australian people had supported an amendment to the Constitution. The pollsters inclined to the view that this proved conclusively that the public approved full civil rights for Aborigines and no further opinion polls have been conducted since.

The cynics commented that these two provisions cost nothing and that in the eastern States the Yes vote increased as it moved further south and the ratio of Aborigines to whites became less: Queensland had an 88 per cent affirmative vote, New South Wales 90 per cent and Victoria 93 per cent. The lowest Yes vote (77 per cent) occurred in the Kalgoorlie electorate of Western Australia, which takes in most of the inland area of that State, including the northwest; and there was an Australia-wide tendency for electorates with a proportionately high Aboriginal population to have a comparatively high No vote.

The last few years have seen a growth in psychological research into culture change among Aborigines and the underlying attitudes leading to that change. E. Sommerlad, in a small-scale study of Sydney and certain country areas in New South Wales,[3] considered the importance of ethnic identification in the integration process and found that a big majority of Aborigines who identified as Australians favoured assimilation, while 80 per cent who identified as Aborigines favoured integration in the two Sydney and two country groups polled: a study of the Aborigines of Mornington Island in the Gulf of Carpentaria concluded that 'neither acquisition nor emulation of western ways has interfered with the old beliefs'[4] Yet in other areas,[5] the traditional environment and the traditional Aboriginal values still persist and limit the development of high individual achievement motivation. Despite its economic disadvantages, the security of living among kin is still preferred to a more precarious life in the major society, where acceptance cannot be assured.

Until just a few years ago, most of the information available on Aboriginal attitudes had come from the anthropologists in their studies of Aboriginal and part-Aboriginal communities throughout Australia, and from these some assessment by Aboriginal groups of their social position can be inferred. Aboriginal communities were found to have certain features in common, both as their situation in the general society and in their own social organization. Most members of these communities, whether urban or rural, were discovered to be living in poverty, with overcrowded and below-standard housing, low level of formal education, lack of work skills, high unemployment or under-employment, occupying a subordinate position in the community as a whole. They form their own sub-culture with adherence to an ethic of mutual aid, rather than to one of upward social mobility as practised in middle-class Australian society. Social interaction is largely among kin and there is strong affiliation to the area of origin. Common law and unstable marriages are frequent and there is more emphasis on the extended and less on the nuclear family than in the general society. Due both to social pressure and discriminatory legislation, past and present, group integration is high and there is a strong feeling of separate identity, even in areas where there is no trace of the traditional Aboriginal culture.

Among the many studies conducted, only two dissenting voices have been raised as to the universality of all these features. Annette Eckermann in Queensland and James

Bell in New South Wales[6] feel that mutual aid and group identity have sometimes been overstressed and that some Aboriginal communities are split by class barriers while others have little feeling of solidarity unless directly attacked from without.

Be that as it may, the same overall features observed so often before in Aboriginal communities were again to be found, in varying degree, in the four towns surveyed here; what it is hoped has been added to the findings is an account of Aboriginal reaction to specific facets of their situation: in particular, a self-assessment of their role and position in the major society.

The four towns, two in Victoria and two in New South Wales, were selected largely as a matter of administrative convenience since they were readily accessible by road or air and contained sufficiently large Aboriginal communities to make their study worthwhile. In addition, the two New South Wales towns had the added interest of quite different reputations with regard to race relations, although they were only twenty miles apart. It is very likely that there are numbers of other towns throughout Australia where Aborigines form a bigger proportion of the population and are in an economic position contrasting more markedly with that of whites, which would have yielded far greater racial tension. But the four towns, lacking drama in their day-to-day racial encounters (though there have been flare-ups from time to time when a threat to the town's equilibrium has been perceived) are calculated to give a picture of the lives of some segments of the Aboriginal population in the 1970s, and of their separation, both voluntary and ascribed, from the major society.

There are formidable barriers to eliciting valid attitudinal information from members of another cultural group. All too often overt questioning will bring evasive or apparently-expected answers; and the participant-observer method is a delicate instrument with which to probe relations between the researcher's and the subjects' races. But the study of social problems cannot wait until more precise

methods of measurement are available and an awareness
of the limitations of the measuring instrument should prevent too great claims to precision being made on its behalf.
With these difficulties borne well in mind, it was felt that
participant-observation would yield more valid data from
Aborigines than could be obtained from a structured questionnaire. There was, however, no reason to doubt the
relative efficiency of a questionnaire in measuring the expressed attitudes of whites. Though some white respondents were guarded in their replies, obviously determined
not to offend against social norms, many assumed that the
interviewer would accept their viewpoint as reasonable and
were unaware that they were attempting to rationalize prejudice, even where this was the case. It must be emphasized,
however, that resultant replies measure what the respondent wished to reveal. The fact that in most racial surveys
the more educated respondent displays less prejudice has
generally been taken to indicate a correlation between education and tolerance. It may also reveal more ability to
mask intolerant views which are not socially acceptable.
Though the neat tables which a structured questionnaire
makes possible appear more scientific than the less precise
generalities of subjective observation, the latter may prove
to be more accurate in the event, since it becomes increasingly more difficult, over a period, to hide felt attitudes
and responses from the trained inquirer.

A questionnaire was administered to a cross-section of
the white population in each town to elicit attitudes towards Aborigines (Appendix I, p. 209). By using this
questionnaire, on the surface as much concerned with
governmental policies and general social attitudes as with
personal feelings towards Aborigines as a group, it was
hoped to obtain relatively frank and revealing replies.

A large number of officials dealing with every facet of
Aboriginal life were interviewed and from them facts and
opinions were obtained as to health, education, housing,
the law, welfare and community matters. Personal contact
was made with the majority of Aboriginal adults in each

town, where possible by chain introduction. The investigator visited Aborigines in their homes by invitation, accompanied them to sporting fixtures, took part in a sewing circle and availed herself of every opportunity of interaction. Sometimes direct questions were asked; mostly the conversation was allowed to flow on its normal course, without additional stimulus. This method always poses ethical problems as to whether information garnered on a personal basis can be published subsequently. To make her position plain, the investigator at the outset of her stay in three of the four towns indicated quite clearly that she had been asked by the Commonwealth government Aboriginal agency to collect information on Aboriginal opinion. In the fourth town, since she was already known to a number of the Aboriginal families, initial introductions were not necessary. A firm assurance was given as to anonymity of the Aboriginal communities concerned and therefore the two New South Wales towns will be designated as Westville and Eastville and the Victorian towns as Northtown and Southtown.

Attitudes, not just of the interviewees but of the investigator, must come under scrutiny in a study such as this. Indignation can be a barrier to understanding and needs to be kept at low pitch. Yet the posture of 'value-free science' cannot be sustained on as emotive a topic as race relations: it is absurd to pretend that the interviewer has no value system, does not feel. The most that he or she can do is to ensure that prejudgement does not cloud the issue, and that the evidence is assessed so as to avoid distortion of the facts. Every effort was made to retain an objectivity of the most rigorous kind commensurate with the humanistic values of justice and concern for those less privileged.

Notes

1. SCHONELL, F. J., *et. al.,* 'The Acceptability of Aboriginal Children in Queensland', *Australian Journal of Psychology*, vol. 7, no. 2, 1955, pp. 121–8.

2. PHILP, H. W. S., 'Prejudice Towards the Australian Aborigine', unpublished Ph.D. thesis, Harvard University, 1958; TAFT, RONALD, 'Attitudes of Western Australians towards Aborigines', in *Attitudes and Social Conditions*, Canberra, 1970; WESTERN, J. S., 'The Australian Aborigine: What White Australians Know and Think About Him – A Preliminary Survey', *Race*, vol. 10, no. 4, pp. 411–34; JENNETT, CHRISTINE, 'Racism and the Rise of Black Power in Australia', M.A. qualifying thesis, University of N.S.W., 1970.

3. SOMMERLAD, E., 'The Importance of Ethnic Identification for Assimilation and Integration: A Study of Australian Aboriginal Attitudes', B.A. Hons. thesis, University of Sydney, 1968.

4. BIANCHI, G. N., *et al.,* 'Cultural Identity and the Mental Health of Australian Aborigines', *Social Science and Medicine*, vol. 3, 1970, pp. 371–85.

5. DAWSON, JOHN L. M., 'Attitude Change and Conflict among Australian Aborigines', *Australian Journal of Psychology*, vol. 21, no. 2, 1969, pp. 101–16.

6. ECKERMANN, A.-K., 'Group Identity and Urban Aborigines', paper presented to Forty-third ANZAAS Congress, Brisbane, 1971; BELL, J., 'The Part-Aboriginal in New South Wales – Three Contemporary Social Situations', in BERNDT, R. and C. (eds.), *Aboriginal Man in Australia*, Sydney, 1965, pp. 396–418.

Chapter Eight

The New South Wales Towns
Yesterday and Today

In the Richmond River area of New South Wales, where two of our towns are situated, clashes between black and white over land were rife from the early days of British settlement, always ending in the withdrawal in disarray of the Aborigines, since their technology was too simple to withstand sophisticated warfare. Retaliation for land usurped was often attempted in the form of Aboriginal seizure of stock and weapons. Cattle 'stealing', castigated and feared by the whites, may have appeared to Aborigines as an easier extension of hunting, white-man's style; while the advantages of European weapons in a situation of seemingly diminishing economic opportunity were obvious: 'They would kill a white man or run the risk of getting shot themselves to get possession of steel axes and tomahawks' commented Mary Bundock, one of the early Richmond River settlers.

From 1814 to 1816 Governor Macquarie used severe military action to defeat the Aborigines of the region, forbidding them to carry weapons or to continue with their 'barbarous' customs. Their leaders were proscribed and exiled and some effort was made to settle them as farmers, always under white supervision. Sporadic raids followed by massive reprisals, the poisoning of flour and attacks on native women became part of a sorry and continuing story. The settlers were outraged by the attacks; the Aborigines were rapidly becoming decimated by murder and disease; it appeared imperative to separate one race from the other. Expeditions of a punitive or protective nature were sent to drive the Aborigines further afield, while government proclamations and general orders were issued forbidding them to come within a certain distance of white settlement. A

Protector was installed in 1838, but was a failure. In fact during his term the Aborigines diminished even more rapidly than before and the whole area was in a state of race war. Decimation was by poison and the gun with the police joining the settlers in the slaughter. By 1849 the Protectorate ceased by order of Governor Gipps, since it had proved a failure. The rule of law as a means of regulating relations between the races had broken down; it was easier to shoot blacks than to bring them to trial.

The Richmond River area was discovered in 1828 by Captain Rous while looking for navigable rivers and better grazing land for drought-stricken sheep farmers in the south. He reported seeing many Aborigines and in the 1840s, Oliver Fry, the Commissioner for Crown Lands, estimated that there were about a hundred on the lower river, where there was a plentiful supply of fish and wild game.

The arrival on the river of the squatters Clay and Stapleton in 1840 marked the end of Aboriginal ownership of the land in the area for, as elsewhere, the squatters assumed a right to the tribal lands without payment of compensation. The cedar cutting and initial pastoral activities did not have a very adverse effect, since stock grazing took place on open pastures and did not diminish the herd of marsupials. But in the 1860s, under Sir John Robertson's *Free Selection Land Act*, great numbers of farmers settled the countryside as agriculturists, and the Aborigines were finally and irrevocably displaced. These farmers proceeded to burn and clear, destroying native flora and fauna, the basis of Aboriginal life. Cattle and sheep, flour and sugar were purloined by the black people and atrocities committed on both sides. One such episode was recorded by Commissioner Fry in 1846, when a hutkeeper on one Richmond River property and two settlers on another were killed by Aborigines and a quantity of flour and bread taken. The *Town and County Journal* some forty years later (28 November 1886) reported the sequel: one hundred men of the tribe were gunned down as a lesson to Aborigines. It is interesting to note that Fry apparently accepted this as an example of frontier justice and does not think it worth mentioning, though he does recount the case of a settler 'killed by a party of Blacks in consequence of going armed to their camp with a view of having improper intercourse with the females'.[1] Not all was venom and destruction, however. A letter to the *Sydney Morning Herald* of 8 July 1842 from Captain Edward Ogilvie, one of the early settlers of the region, was written 'to show the very peaceable disposition and unrevengeful spirit of these people, and to convince those who are in the habit of looking upon them as little better than wild beasts that they are mistaken'.

Nevertheless under these conditions it was inevitable that Aboriginal numbers should diminish through alcohol, disease and malnutrition. Their will to resist was broken. Or, as Robert Leycester Dawson, one of the settlers of the time, expressed it: 'By the seventies they had become quite as amenable to law and order as the average white ... I invariably found them ... ever anxious to please their employer.' The hierarchy had been established, and it was clear on which level Aborigines had landed.

There followed a period of relative calm. Not for the last time in Australia's history did the exigencies of the economic situation dictate a change in race relations. Station owners wanted to employ 'the Blacks' as shepherds, stockmen and domestics and so Aborigines gradually returned to the fringe of settlement and worked for payment in kind. Closer contact with settlers brought about a breakdown of the traditional culture. By 1896 George Sparke, manager of a Richmond River property, is ordering 'slops' (clothes) from a Sydney store for his Aboriginal workers; hunting skill diminishes and the women forget the art of making utensils. Though records remain of wages paid to white and Chinese workers of this era, none exist for Aborigines, who were paid in food, flour and meat and thus became completely subordinate to and dependent on whites. Though the scourge of European disease was high, no record of Aboriginal deaths was recorded in the Death Register of the district court house until the 1890s, a further indication of the invisibility which they already appear to have assumed in white eyes.

It was during this period that the two towns of the survey were founded. Westville was at first the main settlement on the Richmond River. It was the squatters' town, the headquarters of land and police courts, and became a municipality in 1880. Meantime, in 1844, the present site of Eastville was occupied first as a private station, then opened up as a village in 1855. By the time the railway was opened in 1894 Eastville had become the main business centre on the river.

Another Protector of Aborigines was appointed in 1880 and the Aborigines Protection Board, established in 1883, was to help the natives die out peacefully in 'asylums in many districts'. Ninety reserves throughout New South Wales were notified in which Aborigines could live away from whites. This segregation policy remained unchanged until the *Aborigines Protection Act*, 1909. Under this legislation managers of Aboriginal stations were not allowed to supply rations to the able-bodied without special permission from the Board, so that the men would be forced to go out to work and to maintain their families. In 1910 the Board's policy was to remove part-Aboriginal children from the reserves and police were rounding them up for the purpose of bringing them to towns for training. From this era dated the virulent dislike of many Aboriginal families for the government Aboriginal agency. During the depression it was necessary to relax these provisions and permit part-Aborigines to remain on the reserves, since jobs were simply not available. An illustration of how the policy worked in practice may be seen from a brief account of an Aboriginal settlement published in the *Eastville Times*, 6 June 1917:

On Kyogle road, fourteen miles from Westville, nearly every black child has a running nose and infant mortality is very high. It is a pitiful sight to see how spindly-legged and emaciated the Aboriginal children are. Only those parents who have children attending school receive a weekly ration of flour, tea and sugar . . . Sites of Aboriginal camps are bleak and exposed.

Segregation continued through sections of Aboriginal New South Wales over a period of 152 years and still has a profound effect on the Aborigines and part-Aborigines of that State today.

By the 1930s the rationale for the policy of protection by segregation had disappeared. Part-Aborigines, far from dying out, were increasing. The Protection Board was replaced by the Aborigines Welfare Board (which was in the last weeks of its operations at the time of this survey). The legislation of the 1940s[2] changed the emphasis of policy to 'assisting Aborigines to become assimilated into the general life of the community'.[3] The first annual report of the Aborigines Welfare Board to refer to an assimilation policy was that of 1948 which defined its aim as one which would 'make the aborigine a responsible, active, intelligent [sic] citizen'.

The Parliamentary report of 1967,[4] on which the 1969 legislation was to be based, reiterated that 'the policy of assimilation is best for Aborigines'.

Today, Eastville is the centre of one of the most thickly settled rural areas in Australia, and has a population of nearly 19,000; the golden days of winter bring mild sunshine for weeks on end. Dairying and factories based on dairying employ more than a quarter of the neighbouring workforce. But there is a variety of activity in which Eastville's citizens are involved: bananas and sugar, commerce and engineering, textile and printing works all provide both year-round and seasonal employment and all contribute to the thriving town.

Eastville is attractively set in the surrounding hills and is a scene of ceaseless activity. The broad streets are lined with cars and it has already reached the distinction of parking problems. The fact that the town is very much a centre for a district is indicated by the numbers of professional people it supports. The ranks of the middle class are swelled by an adult education centre, Education Department officers and a variety of schools. Orchestral concerts are given regularly in the town hall; there is a local dramatic group and a much-used library. Apart from the stream of neighbouring farmers coming to town for professional and technical advice or for commercial reasons, there is an equally constant stream of travellers stopping in town while en route to other parts. Old-established, cultured and prosperous is Eastville.

Westville, just twenty miles away and with less than half the population (under 9,000) has more the atmosphere of an overgrown village. Physically undistinguished, with its shop-lined main road and with few public buildings of note, it nevertheless exudes an air of quiet civic pride, with well-kept streets and parks, a multitude of sporting organizations, and an airport which makes of it a transport centre. A co-operative meat company and dairy society and a variety of timber mills boost the town's employment but, once again, it is really the surrounding dairying on which it thrives.

Notes

1. *Historical Records of Australia*, 1914, vol. 24, p. 262.
2. *The Aborigines Protection (Amendment) Act* (1940) and *The Aborigines Protection (Amendment) Act* (1943).
3. Section 7(a) of the *Aborigines Protection Act* (1909–43).
4. *Report for the Joint Committee of the Legislative Council and Legislative Assembly Upon Aborigines Welfare*, Part 1, N.S.W., 1967.

Chapter Nine

Aborigines of Eastville and Westville

There are no Aborigines of the full descent in either town; the part-Aborigines of both are predominantly of the Bandjalang tribe and are heavily interrelated. The Aboriginal[1] population of Eastville comprises 142 persons out of a total of 18,600; that of Westville 130 out of 8,200. There is a constant pattern of visiting, largely among kin, either between the two towns, to and from one of the Aboriginal reserves in the district, or to Sydney or Brisbane, which have the attraction of ready employment and all the amenities and glamour of big cities. Those who are young and unmarried, particularly, go to the capital cities for anything from weeks to years, staying with relatives and bringing with them the gossip from their home district.

A study of the Brisbane part-Aboriginal population found that 21 per cent of households had had relatives to stay in the previous year for six weeks or more;[2] while in Sydney[3] visits to the country to stay with relatives were frequent as were also country visitors to city households, with a whole family group often staying for several weeks at a time. Even in a crowded Sydney house it is rare to find members who are not related to the household head.[4] There is considerable interaction with kin and mutual aid with regard to accommodation and child-care in white Australian families also, but this is seldom carried with much intensity beyond the parents' families of origin and their siblings' families, with the number of contacts tending to diminish as class level rises.[5] Even in white working-class areas the sense of community (which Weber described as 'belonging together' and which implies the sharing of a common culture) is not nearly as great as in Aboriginal groups. A recent study of an Adelaide working-class suburb by Jean Martin[6] showed that almost one-third of wives had not visited or been visited by relatives in one week; something which would be inconceivable in our two Aboriginal communities.

Accommodation is readily offered even where conditions are already cramped and income scant. Former country dwellers will go back to their area of origin from time to time for spiritual refreshment and ease or, as they express it, to 'recharge the batteries'. Aborigines of the towns are acutely conscious of their separate identity. When they talk of 'one of our own' they may mean a member of their own extended family or, more probably, any other Aboriginal person. It is obvious that there are two categories of people, 'we' and 'they' and, in time of stress, group cohesion runs high. An example of this occurred at the time of the survey. The (white) head teacher of a primary school, who had gone out of his way to assist Aboriginal children, was robbed. Evidence pointed to the thief's being a visiting, itinerant Aborigine. The teacher inquired of his Aboriginal neighbours, with whom he was on very friendly terms, whether they knew where the miscreant might be, as the police were searching for him. The neighbours, while deploring the thief's behaviour and stressing that he was not connected to them, declared that they had no knowledge of his whereabouts. The teacher later learnt that the wanted man had been in the very house he was visiting while this conversation was going on. He felt himself to be mocked by a group of people whose children he had been helping and whom he had regarded as friends. His wife, distressed at the loss of several hundred dollars' worth of household goods, which had not been insured, urged her husband to give up 'trying to assist those treacherous Abos' and to apply for a transfer to another school. This he gladly consented to do since he felt all his efforts unappreciated and himself betrayed. Yet the condemnation of the thief (for whom there was no personal affection) had been genuine on the Aboriginal side. But it was unthinkable to render to white authority 'one of our own'. This small episode epitomizes the gulf that lies between black and white. Bewilderment and hurt on one side have so often followed seemingly inexplicable actions on the other.

About one-third[7] of Aboriginal households in both towns contain three or more generations, yet there does not appear to be as great a 'generation gap' as in the general run of two-generation white Australian families and certainly not as much conflict as with European migrant households, since the families tend to be non-directive, with a minimum of interference in the actions of the young. There may well be 'inter-personal impoverishment' (to use one of Erikson's terms) among the younger generation. Young people frequently lack guiding principles from their parents, who are caught in a semi-acculturated limbo between two worlds; while the grandparents are geared to a life based on the traditional or the reserve culture. The implications of this inter-generational congruence of attitudes are important: where the parents (and especially the mother) are oriented towards individual upward social mobility, the children are likely to follow. Where the parents reject 'getting ahead' the children are even more likely to be influenced by parental attitudes than are their white counterparts. Table 1 indicates household composition in the two towns.

Table 1

Aboriginal Households, Eastville and Westville

	No. of persons	No. of dwellings	% of total population	% of children under 15*
Eastville	142	24	0·8	49
Westville	130	21	1·5	47

* A survey of Aboriginal areas in New South Wales and Eyre Peninsula, South Australia, showed the proportion of children under fifteen years of age to be 53 per cent (ROWLEY, C. D., 'The Aboriginal Householder', *Quadrant*, November-December, 1967, pp. 90–6).

Education

The general educational level for Aboriginal adults of the two communities is of primary standard, only three households containing one or more adults with some secondary schooling. This reflects previous New South Wales government policy on Aboriginal education which had been kept separate from and inferior to that provided for whites. From the beginning of the century the Protection Board had established schools on reserves, frequently with untrained managers and their wives as teachers, and these were only taken over by the Education Department in 1940. Until this time the syllabus prescribed for Aboriginal schools required children to attain third grade primary standard by the age of fourteen years, a standard generally

Table 2

Education and Occupation, Eastville and Westville (in percentages)

	Education		Occupation of Householder*			
	Not more than primary	At least some secondary	Unskilled, Semi-skilled	Skilled	White Collar	Pension
Eastville:						
Aboriginal	72·4	27·6	36·3	4·5	4·5	54·5
Total	38·3	61·7				
Westville:						
Aboriginal	70·9	29·1	66·5	6·0	0	27·6
Total	41·4	58·6				
Rural Aboriginal, N.S.W.†	70·7	29·2				

* 88 per cent of adults in Brisbane's Aboriginal community had eight or fewer grades of schooling, and 68 per cent had no work skills (BIDDLE, ELLEN H., 'The Assimilation of Aborigines in Brisbane, 1969').

† ROWLEY, C. D., op. cit.

reached by whites at the age of eight. Even after the curriculum change of 1940 one half of school hours had to be spent on manual training, physical education and gardening. Before 1945 no Aboriginal children were permitted to attend State schools, and only from 1949 onwards were all Aboriginal children living away from reserves free to enrol in the general school system. Occupations, accordingly, are all of the unskilled or semi-skilled kind, with only one man trained (as a minister of the church).

Table 3

Secondary School Enrolments, Eastville–Westville Area, August 1969

Form	Ab. students as % of total Aboriginal enrolment N = 37	White students as % of total white enrolment	Mean retardation of Aboriginal Students	
			Years	Months
I	34·4	24·4	0	6
II	47·0	23·0	0	3
III	10·9	19·9	0	5
IV	7·9	19·1	0	4
V	–	7·4	–	–
VI	–	6·0	–	–

In the three High Schools in the Eastville–Westville area students in Forms I and II form 81 per cent of the total Aboriginal enrolment but only 47 per cent of the total white enrolment. Mean length of retardation is four and a half months and there are no Aboriginal students in fifth or sixth form.

Though special Aboriginal scholarships are available to ease the financial burden of secondary schooling, it is obvious that other factors prevent their being put to full use. One of these is the low educational level of parents which prevents their positive evaluation of education. It was noticeable in both Eastville and Westville that many mothers professed aspirations for their children's higher education reflecting a seeming acceptance of the achievement orientation of Australian society, and yet made no effort to prevent their children leaving school at the legal minimum age of fifteen years or, where hardship could be proved or the inspector dodged, fourteen and a half years. This seemingly ambivalent attitude stems from the knowledge that the major society places a high value on education, but a value not accepted by the Aboriginal community, which has tended to eschew the white concept of 'success', partly by choice, partly by necessity. As one mother expressed it: 'You whites have to be *someone* to be accepted by your own kind; we just have to be ourselves.' One often hears the fatalism of 'I wanted Mary to go on with her schooling and be a teacher. But you know what kids are. They just want to be with their pals and out there earning money.'

Poverty and the large-sized household a small income has to support are additional factors in early school-leaving. Even if the adolescent wage-earner has to leave home to get a job and is therefore not a contributor in his parental home, his departure means one less mouth to feed and a fraction less over-crowding.

Aboriginal children usually experience difficulty in understanding a middle-class teacher, who uses an extensive vocabulary and places great reliance in the learning process on the written word. The Aboriginal students of the two towns, like most children brought up in poverty, have only a limited vocabulary and language understanding, and are not part of a literary tradition. Intelligence quotient tests administered to Aboriginal children in Westville High School in 1969 by the New South Wales Education Department disclosed, of a total of sixteen pupils:

2 of very inferior I.Q.
6 of inferior I.Q.
1 of low average I.Q.
6 of average I.Q.
1 of high average I.Q.

The general lowness of scoring was thought by the testers to result from paucity of vocabulary and difficulties in abstract conceptualization which was due, in turn, to their culturally deprived background.

Aboriginal students and their parents frequently accused teachers of anti-Aboriginal bias, which the teachers just as frequently denied. This appeared to be a circular process: the students refused to try, so that they could not be accused of failure; while teachers commented, 'Those dark children are so apathetic it's a waste of time trying to teach them anything.' Aboriginal children band together in the playground, aware from any early age of their separate identity and the low rating of their race in the general community; and act out their defiance of whites in general by refusing to understand the simplest instructions: 'Don't know what you mean, sir.'

The futility of trying is borne out in large measure by employment figures as correlated with educational attainments.[8] For the whole of Australia, these showed that, of 37 Aboriginal women with matriculation, 14 were employed in personal or domestic service; jobs with low status, low pay and little opportunity for advancement. Similarly, of 103 Aboriginal men with matriculation, 79 were blue collar workers. In other words, substantial numbers of Aboriginal matriculants are in occupations where their white counterparts are not to be found and which do not require so high an educational level. Investigations of the position of American blacks have shown striking disparities in employment and income attainment as between black and white. When such variates as family size, education, father's occupation and mental ability are held constant, blacks have significantly lower income than whites. In other words, Negroes are poor mainly because they are Negroes rather than that they have inherited a legacy of poverty.[9]

Aboriginal children are always on the alert for any sign of discrimination from their peers and, like their parents, are super-sensitive to slight. During the time of the survey a Westville mother withdrew her child from school after his school-case had been mutilated by white students. In vain the teachers pleaded that this was a childish feud which could have happened to any white student. The child maintained that he had been under pressure for years because of his colour and could stand no more. 'Those white kids hate us' was his first and final word on the subject. On the other hand, one of the teachers at the Eastville High School was collecting segments of the vernacular language from a student and found the effect on the girl's self-esteem to be marked: for the first time a member of the major society was approaching her as an informant and displaying a respect for her cultural heritage. As a result, her attitude to school began to show increased interest and co-operation.

Aboriginal education is just one more manifestation of the unhealthy relationship which has existed between whites and Aborigines for many decades, and a way will have to be found to alter sharply the paternalism–dependency syndrome which characterizes that relationship. This is most difficult to achieve in a centralized school system where even white, middle-class parents complain that that there is no machinery through which they can express their viewpoint as to curriculum content, discipline or any other facet of school life. Most parent associations act as little more than fund-raising bodies and the schools are seen as child-minders, with a frequent dichotomy of aim between school and home. This is even truer where the home is Aboriginal, with a value system completely at odds with that of the school. Gradually the child gets the message that only through schooling can he prepare himself for adulthood in society: that what is learned outside school is not worth knowing. This is what the educationist Ivan Illich has called the 'hidden curriculum of schooling' which applies as well, of course, to whites.

In recent years compensatory programmes, especially remedial English and arithmetic, were thought to be the best method of bringing the underprivileged child up to the expected standard. But lately, educators have been coming to the conclusion that a child learns when he can see the self-relevance of that learning, not because programmed instruction is being fed to him in an easily assimilable form. Thus education begins from the practical, the task-oriented, and fans out from there along the lines of the child's own interests; no longer divided into the tightly knit disciplines of history, arithmetic, science and the like, but roaming into the broad fields of the student's current enthusiasms with supporting relevant information available from teacher and school.

Instead of building educational programmes around deficits (on the basis that the Aboriginal child is likely to be deficient in the intricacies of middle-class language, for instance) they can be built on strengths. The child of poverty is what Riessman[10] called a 'physical' learner, one who responds more to visual and auditory techniques with which he has constantly been bombarded outside school and with which he is far more at ease than with the abstract verbal mode of the middle class. This is not to say that he must always be kept at that level and will never be able to enter the field of academic studies. If he is allowed to follow his own path of learning and is assisted by largely audio-visual teaching, he can make use of the co-operative methods to which he is accustomed rather than the competitive ones of the examination system, with its inbuilt fear of failure. With each competent performance of the student will come an increase in his self-image as a competent person. Early success leads to increased skills and knowledge and so to increased self-esteem, whereas early failure brings in its train hesitancy and a sense of powerlessness.[11] In 1966 the Coleman report on *Equality of Educational Opportunity* reviewed the achievement of hundreds of thousands of American school children, black and white, and found that the feeling of ability to control the environment was the variable which showed the strongest relationship to educational achievement. The achievement of children from the disadvantaged groups, in particular, appeared closely related to what they believed about their environment: whether it would respond to reasonable effort on their part or whether it was merely random or immovable. The child whose parents are poor, who lives in a slum, who is constantly buffeted by fate and made to feel his power-lessness cannot be expected to have acquired motivation to achieve. Where society is seen as indifferent or threatening, lack of self-direction and resistance to change are likely to become the central values of such children, whose low educational aspirations are realistic. Schools which stress initiative and curiosity will help the child discover the relevance to himself of what he learns, even where there is little in the home background to reinforce this newly found confidence. The personality and character of the individual will grow with the subsequent achievement of self-realization and identity: by observing that he is able to perform tasks competently, he will become a more self-reliant and self-assured person.

But is a high level of formal education necessary for success in the general community? At first glance, it would appear from the lives of many whites in the country towns that this is not so. From those who left school at the age of twelve or thirteen, we have an owner of four taxis, an affluent farmer, a chairman of Rotary and a city councillor. All in a sound economic position, all well respected in their town. But the opportunities for self-advancement without education decrease with time, as the general educational level of the community increases. It is estimated by the Australian Council for Educational Research that by 1975 40 per cent of seventeen-year-olds will be staying on at school, and 65 per cent of sixteen-year-olds. Compared with this upsurge, Aboriginal figures for secondary education in New South Wales, as disclosed in a New South Wales Teachers' Federation survey of 1971, are markedly low. There were only twelve Aboriginal students in sixth form in the whole State, out of a total Aboriginal secondary enrolment of 1,600. Compared with the State-wide average of one in fifteen in Form 6, the number of Aboriginal sixth-formers should have been 108, nine times as many. In addition, 38 per cent of Aboriginal secondary students were in slow-learner classes. The Teachers' Federation suggests that one remedy to a highly unsatisfactory situation would be the inclusion in teachers' college curricula of special courses on teaching Aboriginal and other culturally different children; and that teachers should acquire as part of their training some background in Aboriginal culture and history, not just of the traditional society, but also of part-Aborigines, with whom many of them may come in contact. Aboriginal history and treatment have been vastly different from that of whites and they will therefore think and react along different lines from their white classmates. Small wonder that their conduct frequently baffles teachers, untrained as to its cause. Additionally, Aboriginal students resent the fact that all their teaching concerns a society other than their own. Australian history only begins in 1770: complete cultural homogeneity is assumed and white middle-class values prevail. As an Aboriginal identity has expressed it: 'We go to school, but all we are taught about our country is what the white people have done.'[12]

The fact that the figures had only improved marginally since the Federation's previous survey in 1964 would indicate that attention has only been paid to extrinsic motivational factors such as the provision of scholarships, and not enough to intrinsic factors such as the raising of the Aboriginal self-image, increased autonomy of the Aboriginal student to pursue the lines of his own interests, encouragement to succeed by co-operation and not competition, and assistance with auditory and visual aids in order to expand competence and therefore self-confidence. As with the Australian education system as a whole, it is not so much a question of repairing an antiquated edifice by patching it with more of the same bricks, but by taking an analytical look at the structure as it stands and using it to the greater advantage of the individual student.

Employment

Education is considered by black and white communities alike as being more important for vocational training than for personality development, and there is little incentive to higher education in the shortage of employment of the entire area, which has the highest percentage of unemployment benefits for the whole of New South Wales. Many of the whites interviewed refused to concede that the high rate of unemployment among Aborigines was due to anything but malingering on their part. 'If they really wanted jobs, they'd find them.' The *Report on Income Maintenance Programs*, commissioned by the President of the United States in 1969, is relevant here:

With so many working at jobs that are both unpleasant and financially unrewarding, one wonders how the stereotype of the malingering poor can be sustained. It is wrong that so much attention is focussed on the few laggards ... Very few of those capable of self-help seem to be doing nothing.

Aborigines tend to work in seasonal employment on sugar-cane, millet and maize harvesting, cane-planting and stripping. All of this work, apart from being seasonal, is dependent on weather, availability and transport. A few gain jobs in the meat-works or railways and one works for the Eastville City Council. The same shortage of employment prevails in both Eastville and Westville, with Aborigines tending to get poorly paid work unwanted by whites. Many have a tentative attitude towards applying for employment, since they feel sure that prejudice will prevent their getting it. In the event, it is a rare employer who, confronted with an Aborigine and a white applicant of equal competence, gives the job to the former. One Westville farmer was reported as having obtained a consistently satisfactory work record from his Aboriginal employees over a period of many years. When asked why this was, when farmers all about him complained of unreliability and laziness, he replied: 'It's like this, see: I treat them like human beings. I like them. They like me. I don't go in for any of them fancy incentive payments. I just pay the award and they do a fair day's work for it.' His assessment was confirmed by his Aboriginal farmhands: 'He's a decent sort of cove and he trusts us.'

Employment opportunities are especially lacking for those under twenty-one years of age and for females; hence the tendency for girls to stay at school longer than boys. Sometimes this 'sitting it out' at school is a source of irritation to teachers, since it is obviously not motivated by desire to learn but helps fill in an endless amount of free time. Two pretty young sisters, aged fifteen and sixteen, were visited in Eastville. They had spent the morning helping their mother with the household chores, and then dressed themselves attractively, with great attention to cosmetic detail, and were just sitting on the verandah when the interviewer called. She was obviously the event of the day, and they did their utmost to detain her with information, both real and apocryphal, about the local community. In the evening, they would go to the park to meet the local Aboriginal boys. There was no possibility of any sort of job in the vicinity and they had begun to pester their mother to allow them to go to Sydney. Although she maintained that they were too young to live so far away, it was obvious that she would shortly succumb to pressure and let them go. Another year spent in school would not have altered the situation since there would still be no jobs; another year of doing nothing in the town was likely to end in early pregnancy.

Housing

During the course of interviewing in private homes in Eastville and Westville a (subjective) assessment of housekeeping standards and also of the physical level of each dwelling was made. This disclosed a marked difference between the two towns as to housekeeping ability, which must be taken as one of the acculturation criteria. 'Condition of House' (Table 4) refers to structural inadequacies such as badly cracked walls, lack of water or electricity, shack construc-

Table 4

Housing, Eastville and Westville

	Total Occupied Dwellings	Owner of Dwelling % Govt. Agency	Other	Mean No. of Rooms*	Housekeeping % Good	Fair	Poor	Condition of House % Good	Fair	Poor	Mean No. of Persons per Dwelling†	Occupancy Status† % Own	% Rent
Eastville:													
Aboriginal	24	37·5	62·5	4·0	58·3	20·8	20·8	37·5	29·2	33·3	5·9	9·5	90·5
General§	5,190	–	–	6·0	–	–	–	–	–	–	3·6	79·0	21·0
Westville:													
Aboriginal	21	19·1	80·9	3·8	85·7	9·5	4·7	42·8	28·5	28·5	6·1	17·6	82·4
General§	2,303	–	–	5·8	–	–	–	–	–	–	3·7	78·8	21·2

* The mean number of rooms per dwelling was 4·6 in Aboriginal Brisbane (BIDDLE, op. cit.).

† The mean number of persons per dwelling was 5·6 for Aboriginal Brisbane; 7·0 for Aboriginal rural New South Wales (ROWLEY, op. cit.), and 8·6 for Aboriginal Sydney (LICKISS op. cit.).

‡ 76 per cent of household units in Brisbane occupied rented housing, 41·5 per cent in rural New South Wales. The figure for the total population of rural New South Wales is 33 per cent.

§ Commonwealth Census, 30 June 1966.

tion, and general state of dilapidation. The number of persons per dwelling was calculated without regard for visitors, though in effect the majority of households receive regular visits from kin, which add to the overcrowding and to the difficulties of housekeeping both from the hygienic and budgetery standpoints. It is completely unheard of for an Aborigine to stay at a hotel or boarding house. The low housekeeping standards of the Eastville Aboriginal community result from recent occupancy of the meanest shacks on a reserve, and from a low educational level. This whole housing table adds up to a picture of poverty: small, dilapidated and overcrowded houses, in which the occupants, as tenants, have very little stake. Norelle Lickiss,[13] commenting on Aboriginal households in Sydney, observed a similar situation:

There was very little attempt to decorate the dwelling in any way. The exterior was frequently neglected, left unpainted or untidy, with no concern for appearance ... Family photographs were occasionally displayed, likewise sporting trophies and other emblems ... Otherwise there was little sign of the personal influence of the occupants upon the dwelling.

At the time of the survey new legislation had been introduced into the New South Wales parliament, known as the *Aborigines Act*, 1969, which was to dissolve the Aborigines Welfare Board and to substitute a Directorate of Aboriginal Welfare which would operate within the Department of Child Welfare and Social Welfare. Under this new Act provision was to be made for the administration of Aborigines Welfare Board houses to pass to the Housing Commission. Great uneasiness was expressed by Aborigines at the proposed change, since it was felt that those behind in their rent were likely to be evicted. Families living on social service payments or with only sporadic employment maintained that it was impossible to set aside money for rental. Fear of being without a roof was considerable and was frequently discussed.

Health

A white observer has commented on the New South Wales scene:

In seven years of daily contact with Aborigines I was never once approached for advice on how to attain or retain health. Aborigines are interested in being cured when ill, but health as such does not concern them. This should not surprise us if we have any knowledge of health extension work in our own community. We, like the Aborigines, do not seek health positively, but concern ourselves with the curing of disease.[14]

Medical workers in both towns accept as inevitable a lower standard of general health for the Aboriginal community.

Studies of infant birth-weights in various rural areas of New South Wales indicate that there is a high percentage of Aboriginal children born who weigh less than six pounds and that this is likely to be due to the mother's inadequate diet. The Aboriginal maternal mortality rate is also higher than for whites. Malnutrition and respiratory infections, which are correlated with low educational and living standards, are prevalent. There is a general dietary deficiency of vegetables and citrus fruit and a resultant lack of vitamin C. It is now known that early malnutrition has a bearing on mental function, the evidence pointing to a critical period of growth of the central nervous system during which malnutrition, even in a mild form, may produce irreversible damage. This critical period, when rapid cell division normally takes place, extends from the pre-natal period to the end of the child's first year.

Aborigines were convinced that there was prejudice against them from the staff of the Westville hospital, and tried to avoid going there. At one stage (approximately fifteen years ago) there had been segregated wards for Aborigines and the fear of discrimination may have been residual to those times. Individual members of staff have also displayed some distaste for or sharpness with Aboriginal patients which the latter, not unnaturally, are quick to feel and to resent. Accusations of prejudice on the part of the local medical officer were constantly expressed. This doctor, Aborigines maintained, refused to endorse claims for invalid pensions where these were valid, thus forcing them to domicile themselves temporarily in another area to obtain essential social service benefits. This same medical officer expressed his view on Aborigines in the most forthright terms, while being questioned as to Aboriginal health statistics: 'Hitler had the right idea! Adult Aborigines are a hopeless lot. They should all be sent to the gas-chambers, then maybe we could do something with the children.' Like the true racist that he was, he later qualified his remarks by mentioning that several part-Aboriginal families were among his Westville patients; that these were 'only quarter-caste and not bad types'. His comments were passed on to a white executive member of the Aborigines' Advancement League who dismissed them by saying, 'Dr —— and I don't see eye to eye on Aborigines but we're good friends just the same. Apart from this little peculiarity he's a nice man.' The peculiarity did not seem so little to Aborigines who had to come, cap in hand, to request a medical certificate, who could feel his animosity and knew that they were likely to be summarily dismissed without one. Resentment was also expressed against the local Health Inspector who could, legally, enter an Aborigines Welfare Board house without a warrant, though he could not do so with other houses.

Religion

The Pentecostalism previously observed among the Bandjalang[15] no longer has such a marked influence on the people of Eastville and Westville, who tend to go to the established churches in the town, or to no church at all. Pentecostalism is an arm of Christianity which lays stress

on 'the gift of the Holy Ghost' and has its external manifestation in 'speaking in tongues'. Those so invested with
powers by the Holy Ghost can perform healing rites in
much the same way as the 'clever men' of the Old Law
could do. It sprang up in several countries at the beginning
of this century, spreading among the dispossessed, who
could expect to be compensated in the next life, and providing an alternative value system to that of the major
society. The humble are to sit on the right hand of God,
the powerful are rejected. The reserve, which until 1963
existed five miles from Eastville (and which will be called
Eastville reserve from here on) contained a church presided
over by an Aboriginal pastor, which practised Pentecostalism. Revivalist meetings are still held regularly on other
nearby reserves and are attended by the townspeople. The
emotional satisfaction which these regional meetings give
is nowadays more related to the reinforcement of kinship
ties and feelings of group identity than to their purely religious content, though the latter undoubtedly provides
some comfort. A white woman who interacts constantly
with Aborigines commented drily that the Bandjalang of
the two towns, feeling themselves oppressed by their continuously subordinate position, were forced to turn to either
an alcoholic or a Pentecostal solution. What Pentecostalism
remains in Eastville and Westville is an integrating factor
within the Bandjalang community, tending to cut Aborigines off from the major town society, which adheres to
more orthodox sects.

Attitude to Institutions for Aborigines

Attitudes expressed towards the Aborigines Welfare Board
indicated a deep-lying resentment of the Board as a representative of the major society and therefore of injustice and
oppression. This feeling goes back to the time when part-
Aboriginal children were taken away from their parents for
training elsewhere and adults were subject to severe repres-

sion and discrimination; and partly it is engendered by the constant and humiliating encounters with white authority today. Aborigines have an understandable indignation at their own lack of resources, both economic and technical, and their frequent exposure to white bureaucrats against whose decisions there is no appeal, however arbitrary they may appear.

Aloofness or even animosity towards the Board's Welfare Officer was shown, especially by adolescents. Several Aborigines expressed the view that help should not be accepted from the government. One mother commented: 'I'm not going to take one of their scholarships for my kids. Who do they think we are? Poverty-stricken or something? We'll make our own way.' A moment later she added: 'It's disgraceful that the Board doesn't provide decent housing for us. Or at least it should repair its rotten houses. They think anything is good enough for us dark people.' Inconsistency marks feelings on both sides of the colour bar.

The Westville Aborigines Advancement League received limited Aboriginal backing; once again, it was seen largely as a white organization since it had a predominance of white members, who interacted with Aborigines on an unequal level. A public meeting called by the Aborigines Advancement League to consider the opening of an Aboriginal Centre in Westville was well attended by both whites and Aborigines and there was general support for the idea by Aborigines, though this support was tempered with concern as to how 'they' (the whites) would run it, and a fear that it might be regarded in the town as a charitable organization. In the event, this fear was to be justified, since the white committee members, even when in a minority, tended to have a dominating influence.

There was general awareness of the annual meetings of the national body, FCAATSI, for which local representatives were appointed each year. The information rendered from these meetings brought a consciousness of other Aboriginal communities and widened the scope of group integration. The increase in knowledge of the problems of other

Aboriginal groups led to more interest in news items and television programmes concerning Aborigines in general although, not surprisingly, attention was more concentrated on local than on far-distant events.

Some pride and a more than usual degree of enthusiasm were displayed in describing the Aboriginal Family Education Centre on a reserve twenty miles away, the primary aim of which is the growth in Aborigines of their self-concept. The Centre was open two half-days a week for pre-school-age children, and was staffed by the parents, with professional support and training from the University of Sydney Department of Adult Education, who issued certificates at different levels to parents who had attended discussion, videotape and film programmes and had traversed specially written material to enable them to guide their children both within the Centre and at home. There was interaction between parents of a number of these groups throughout New South Wales, and the children had shown themselves eager for learning experience. What engendered the enthusiasm for this, as distinct from other avenues of learning, was the fact that the Centre was actually run by Aboriginal mothers, albeit with outside support. This institution was 'ours' whereas almost everything else was 'theirs'; responsibility had been thrown into the Aboriginal camp and, despite the vicissitudes of depressed economic conditions, sub-standard housing, large families, illness, factionalism and doubt as to ability, there was pride in Aboriginal achievement and in the confidence vouchsafed them.

Aboriginal Culture

Although only five households in Eastville and three in Westville professed to knowledge of the Bandjalang language, in most families even among the young people a few phrases of the vernacular survive and derogatory remarks can be murmured against whites, or jokes shared, without the latter being aware of them. These language remnants are used not so much for added ease of expression, since English is the native tongue of both Aboriginal communities, but as a means of group cohesion and white exclusion. The word *dugai* (originally 'stinking corpse') is used generally as a synonym for whites, though *mada* (master), still prevalent in the 1950s, has been dropped. There has been for some years a tendency to regard 'Aborigine' as a term of opprobrium, since it was always used in this context by whites, and 'the dark people' is substituted in its stead. Quite recently accommodation has had to be made to the fact that Aboriginal urban dwellers have begun to refer to themselves as 'blacks', but this term was not tolerated in the towns at the time of the survey.

The slight but growing interest in Aboriginal art on the part of whites was reflected in the glimmerings of resurgent pride in traditional arts and crafts. A manifestation of this is seen on a nearby reserve where both Aborigines of the full descent and part-Aborigines reside. Traditional dances had virtually died out but are now being revived and performed for racially mixed audiences, outside the reserve. Among the older people there is still a strong feeling for the *jurraveel* or totemic site from which a Bandjalang draws his feeling of belonging and there is a reluctance to take any white to view such sites, which are held sacred. An elderly Aborigine who had been describing some of the traditional spiritual practices remembered from his youth made it quite plain that sacred sites were never shown to whites, for fear that they might be desecrated. Many of the younger members of the Aboriginal community were oblivious as to their whereabouts. There is also adherence among the older people to belief in the traditional 'clever men' who could heal by physical contact and could also prevent illness and harm by warning of situations to avoid. A recent study of attitudes among three Aboriginal groups[16] concluded that there was still unresolved conflict of attitude among certain Aboriginal groups over such items as magic and 'clever men' in which they were enjoined by their upbringing to believe, while at the same time being aware that whites jeered at such notions as superstition. But it is not just common cultural traditions or a common language which binds Aboriginal groups together; equally important are awareness of a common history, linkage through kinship and the tension of being part of an impotent minority constantly pressurized by the powerful major society.

Attitudes to White Society

As one would expect, Aborigines living in the towns have achieved a higher degree of acculturation, are more 'westernized' than those on the reserves. Motivation for moving to the towns is usually a search for better housing and employment opportunities, a chance to move up the socio-economic scale. Mr Bert Groves, a representative of the Aboriginal Progress Association, at a conference of North Coast Aborigines at Westville in March 1969, said that the towns of the area 'were not friendly places for Aborigines to live in'. He went on to point out that for this very reason, a continuation of the reserves was essential as a place of retreat for those who could not withstand town hostility. A father who had recently moved to Eastville remarked bitterly:

To live in town we have to be perfect. If my little boy runs around without clothes on, the whites shrug and say 'What do you expect? He's gone native.' If my wife lets the house get a bit untidy the white neighbours will mutter about 'Abo ways'. So she's always in there cleaning and tidying so as they won't have anything to say against her.

Another family living on a nearby reserve complained of the lack of work and sub-standard housing with which they had perpetually to contend. The wife said:

We left the reserve once and moved into town. We had a beaut house and my husband could nearly always find work.

107

But we nearly died of loneliness. No one to drop in for a chat and a cup of tea; no one to help when the kids were sick. We just couldn't stand that sort of living any more, so we packed up and came back to this [pointing with disfavour to the ramshackle house]. At least here among our own we feel we exist.

There is a general feeling among Aborigines that they are judged by a more rigorous and idealized standard than are whites and that acceptance can never be taken for granted.

At the same time, they either share or feel they ought to share some of these standards, even though they are identity-denying. A mother of twelve children declared: 'I love the lot; even the dark ones who are like their old man. Of course six of them are light-skinned like me. You'd hardly call them dark folk at all' (with an air of pride). Several parents stated, almost as soon as the investigator crossed the threshold: 'My kids have never been in trouble with the police. We don't drink, you know, and we don't owe anybody anything. We're decent, law-abiding citizens, and we keep ourselves to ourselves.' Any white is seen as a would-be upholder of community mores, come to enforce them on black people. With the ever-present stereotype of an Aborigine as unreliable, dirty and feckless, possible attack is warded off by defence from the Aboriginal side.

Aborigines of the two towns regarded police as instruments of tyranny, and considered that they were blamed unjustly for whatever crimes were committed. They also maintained that their homes were entered by police without a search warrant. Indeed, one of the fears over the new *Aborigines Act* was that it would declare reserves to be public places, thus permitting police to enter without a warrant. When describing their life as an Aboriginal family living in the town, more than one householder concluded an account of daily routine with the words 'and we always keep out of trouble', as though this were the most positive achievement that could be accomplished. Moreover, the words are usually uttered with an underlying anxiety, since this happy state of affairs might not continue indefinitely. Bertrand Russell once remarked that there are two categories of people: those who feel safer when policemen are about and those who feel less safe. It is obvious into which category Aborigines fall.

A perusal of recent police records in both towns showed that the big majority of charges were for drunkenness or offences relating to alcohol. The police maintained that there was no bias shown against Aborigines; and Aborigines were equally adamant that whereas white inebriates would be escorted home by the police with a warning 'don't do it again', they themselves would invariably be charged and sentenced.

There is a tendency for whites to regard Aborigines as though they did not exist. More than one white respondent, when being questioned as to his opinion on Aborigines in Eastville, expressed astonishment that there *were* any Aborigines in Eastville (despite the fact that they may be seen in the town every day of the week and are, in appearance, clearly identifiable). One is reminded of the episode where Huckleberry Finn accounts to Aunt Sally for his lateness by inventing an accident aboard a river-boat:

'We blowed out a cylinder head.'

'Good gracious! Anybody hurt?'

'No'm. Killed a nigger.'

'Well, it's lucky, because sometimes people do get hurt.'

The Aboriginal response is to live up to this concept of invisibility. Particularly in Eastville, they do not linger in town longer than is necessary, nor do they make more than the essential minimal contacts with whites or their institutions. It was not possible to investigate all of Eastville's seventy-three voluntary organizations as to their Aboriginal membership, but it was obvious that this was extremely low, even in comparison with white manual workers, among whom there is a general tendency to take relatively little part in voluntary associations.[17] It has been found that European immigrants become members of Australian voluntary groups through personal contacts and friendships with Australian workmates and neighbours.[18] On the whole, there is little meaningful social interaction between black and white, and real friendships across the colour line are rare, which no doubt accounts for Aboriginal reluctance to join clubs and societies in which their welcome would be doubtful and they would not feel at ease.

Recent Events

No single event in Eastville's history has roused more conflicting emotions than the closure of the Aboriginal reserve six miles from the town. Since the early 1930s this had been constantly occupied by an Aboriginal group who had not so much 'settled' but had been chased there from their original settlement on the other side of the river. Living (or 'existing') conditions on the reserve were appalling. Fifteen families occupied home-built tumbledown shacks without reticulated water, sewerage, electricity, or garbage disposal. The ground was a sea of mud in winter, a whirl of dust in summer and it was impossible to keep the shacks clean. The only water available was taken from the Richmond River in which an occasional dead cow was seen to float past. Because of the badly polluted water, the Health Department since 1955 had been requesting that some action be taken. Had this been a white community (though it is highly unlikely that it would have been pushed onto such a woeful living space in the first place) action would have been forthcoming instantly, particlularly as infant mortality was high, due to the excessively unhygienic conditions. But this was not a white community and the general public has become accustomed to low standards of housing and services for its black citizens which it would not tolerate on such an apparent and wholesale scale for whites.

A small band of concerned white citizens formed a committee in 1957 and called a first public meeting to take up the appeal for closure of the reserve. The committee struggled on for a short time but was soon forced to close down because of lack of public interest. In 1960 the Eastville Trades and Labor Council made representations to the Aborigines Welfare Board, the Shire Council, the Minister for Health and the Eastville City Council, as did the local Aborigines Advancement League two years later. The League had been formed in 1961 with the primary purpose of moving Aborigines from the reserve, but it set about obtaining publicity for the whole situation in both the local and the national press. As a result of this long agitation the Aborigines Welfare Board decided to buy land in the town on which to build fifteen houses for the reserve dwellers. At its meeting early in 1962 the Eastville City Council refused to sell the land, one alderman stating that 'Council must face the fact that Aborigines are outcasts' and the old argument was advanced that property values would drop around the proposed new Aboriginal area and the ratepayers just would not stand for it. His assessment of public opinion was not altogether incorrect. Three days later, at a public meeting in Eastville called by the Aborigines Advancement League to discuss the matter, feelings ran high, in fact they bordered on the hysterical – particularly on the part of those whose properties adjoined the proposed Aboriginal area. One speaker maintained that 'Nobody's wife or child will be safe coming home after dark if Aborigines are allowed into the town.' However, after hours of stormy debate (from a meeting that had been somewhat stacked by the League) the final vote favoured town housing. The local Council was not to be moved by mere democratic procedures. A full seven months after this meeting the Government Whip in the New South Wales Legislative Assembly stated that the Welfare Board had been trying to buy land in Eastville for the past twenty years but had always met with steady refusal from the City Council.

Adverse publicity continued in the Sydney press, which deplored the callousness of Eastville. Towards the end of 1962 the Minister for Public Works announced that six of

111

the reserve families would be settled just outside the town on two acres of land. The local community was not going to let itself be bulldozed by outside authority. The engineer of the local Shire Council predicted that 'there will probably be some very strenuous objections by ratepayers to the Board's plans.' The patience of the Aborigines Advancement League was beginning to run out: what they had tried but failed to gain at the front door they would now snatch at the back. An area of land half a mile beyond the city limits was bought by the president of the League in his own name and then immediately resold without profit to the Welfare Board. The site was an unattractive one outside town limits and opposite a car dump. 'Every time I pass that place', an Aborigine commented, 'it just drives home the point that the whites don't like us polluting their town. We're unwanted, useless people, stuck away out of sight among the unwanted, useless, cars.' Five houses were built and one bought on the site. The remaining six reserve families were scattered in other areas.

The controversy that the rehousing aroused was reflected in letters to the editor of the *Eastville Times*. The town had been stirred and feelings ran high on every side. One typical letter referred to the Aborigines' 'enormous task to rise to our white standard of living' and concluded with, 'Let us white folk endeavour to lift up the fallen'. Another letter of the same date declares that 'Few people give a damn what happens to their dark brothers.' The line between paternalism and racism has ever been thin.

Concurrently with the reserve fracas had been a smaller controversy at a coastal resort, Beachtown, some thirty miles from Eastville.

The owner of a house there had objected to the Aborigines Welfare Board's settling an Aboriginal family in the town, again on the basis that it would cause land values to fall. His objection was taken up by the Beachtown Progress Association and supported by the Beachtown Council. This, too, was reported fully in the Eastville press.

For the Aboriginal families who moved, apprehensively, into the town, their troubles were far from over. The first family was chosen for its adherence to the town's mores. The husband was a steady worker and keen gardener, the wife an excellent housekeeper and attentive mother. A quiet, shy woman, she later told of the agonies which she had suffered in the first few months in the new house. At first she had had been elated at what to her seemed like a mansion, with all the features of which she had dreamed on the reserve: hot water, electricity, sewerage, an adequate bathroom and kitchen. But, after moving in, she was constantly made fearful of people unknown chalking invective of the 'Blacks get out' variety on the outside walls and throwing rubbish over the back fence. 'We would have got out, too, if we'd had anywhere else to go', she later confessed. After a time the nuisance ceased and one or two of the neighbours would stop her in the street for a chat. Not surprisingly, her response was pleasant and polite – but reserved. Her husband's wry comment was: 'First we're the street's enemies. Then they decide they're going to be our friends. Maybe by tomorrow something else will crop up, and they'll decide they don't want us again.'

Two of the outstanding characteristics of Aborigines in both Eastville and Westville were their sensitivity to criticism and their defeatism when faced with even the possibility of white competition. This latter point was illustrated by an Aboriginal couple who had been trying for some months, but without avail, to procure a low-rental house in Eastville which they needed urgently. Eventually, through an estate agent, they found one and were accordingly elated. But as soon as they knew that a white family was interested in the house, they ceased contact with the agent and were downcast at yet another failure. The husband had a steady job and references as to their reliability as tenants. When they were urged by the investigator to pursue their interests with the agent, they just muttered, 'What's the use? As if he and the owner wouldn't prefer a white to a dark tenant any day!'

The sensitivity to rebuff is constantly being fed by well-publicized accounts of discrimination in the district. One episode discussed in the Aboriginal community was a press interview with the matron of a children's home, in the course of which she stated that an Aboriginal child in the home, though physically perfect, was less likely to be adopted than a white child, despite the fact that 70 per cent of the latter had physical defects.

Another item which gave rise to considerable resentment, tinged with resignation, concerned an allegation in the local newspaper in early 1969 that a Rugby Association was adopting an 'apartheid policy' towards a largely Aboriginal team in the district which, though highly successful, had none of its members chosen to play in a major match.

A further event at the time of the survey concerned an effort to evict most of the Aboriginal community at a small north coast town, despite the fact that they had lived in the area and had been self-supporting for eighty years. A public meeting and television publicity caused the Minister for Lands to rescind the decision, but the whole episode added to the feeling of insecurity and powerlessness which affects the entire community.

It is this tentative approach which is one of the most striking features of the Aborigines of Eastville and Westville. Never sure of where or whether they will find acceptance, economically insecure, lacking the reserves with which to cope with sudden mischance such as illness or accident, they are on the outskirts of the town in spirit even though they may physically live in its centre. The strengths of Aboriginal living lie in the strong feeling of community, of an 'interdependence of fate' which they share among themselves and which stretches out along the kinship network into the surrounding countryside. Despite faction fighting, which undoubtedly exists, and occasional squabbling within the family, there still remains a strong group spirit which is used to battling in corporate fashion and will continue to do so, often with great reserves of ingenuity and dry humour.

Notes

1. In referring to the four towns the word 'Aborigine' will be used to indicate part-Aborigines.

2. BIDDLE, ELLEN H., 'The Assimilation of Aborigines in Brisbane 1965', Ph.D. thesis, University of Missouri.

3. LICKISS, J. NORELLE, 'Aboriginal Children in Sydney: The Socio-Economic Environment', *Oceania*, vol. 41, no. 3, pp. 201–27.

4. BEASLEY, PAMELA, 'The Aboriginal Household in Sydney', in *Attitudes and Social Conditions*, Canberra, 1970.

5. FALLDING, H., 'Inside the Australian Family', in ELKIN, A. P. (ed.), *Marriage and the Family in Australia*, Sydney, 1957, p. 59; BRYSON, LOIS and THOMPSON, FAITH, *An Australian Newtown: Life and Leadership in a Working-Class Suburb*, Melbourne, 1972; MARTIN, JEAN, 'Extended Kinship Ties: An Adelaide Study', *Australian and New Zealand Journal of Sociology*, vol. 3, no. 1, 1967.

6. MARTIN, JEAN, op. cit.

7. 33 per cent in Eastville, 29 per cent in Westville.

8. BROOM, LEONARD, 'Workforce and Occupational Statuses of Aborigines', *Australian and New Zealand Journal of Sociology*, vol. 7, no. 1, 1971.

9. DUNCAN, OTIS DUDLEY, 'Inheritance of Poverty or Inheritance of Race', in MOYNIHAN, D. (ed.), *On Understanding Poverty,* New York, 1968, pp. 85–110.

10. RIESSMAN, F., cited in MCLENDAN, J. C., *Social Foundations of Education*, New York, 1969, p. 39.

11. This theory has been propounded by, among others, BREWSTER-SMITH, M., 'Competence and Socialization', in CLAUSEN, J. A., *Socialization and Society*, Boston, 1968, Chapter 7.

12. WATSON, LEN, *Identity*, vol. 5, no. 4, April 1972.

13. LICKISS, J. NORELLE, op. cit., pp. 204–5.

14. HAUSFELD, R. G., 'Aborigines in New South Wales', *Australian Quarterly*, vol. 37, no. 3, p. 73.

15. CALLEY, MALCOLM J. C., 'Aboriginal Pentecostalism:
A Study of Changes in Religion, North Coast, New South
Wales', unpublished M.A. thesis, University of Sydney,
1955; Pentecostalism Among the Bandjalang', in REAY,
MARIE, (ed.), *Aborigines Now*, Sydney, 1964, pp. 48–58.

16. DAWSON, JOHN L. M., 'Attitude Change and Conflict
Among Australian Aborigines', *Australian Journal of
Psychology*, vol. 21, no. 2, 1969, pp. 101–16.

17. BRENNAN, THOMAS, *Reshaping a City*, Glasgow, 1959.

18. ZUBRZYCKI, J., *Settlers of the Latrobe Valley*, Canberra, 1964, p. 142.

Chapter Ten

The Victorian Towns
Yesterday and Today

The infiltration of Victoria by Europeans proceeded on similar lines to those of New South Wales, but at a later date. Exploration began in 1802 and in 1835 Governor Arthur of Tasmania sent what amounted to an expedition to Port Phillip to found a colony; it was the same Arthur who, despite his own protests, had been forced by the settlers to exile the last of the Tasmanian Aborigines to inhospitable islands in Bass Strait. John Batman, who led the expedition, drew up a document along the lines of a number of American Indian treaties, in which he exchanged flour, blankets, knives, tomahawks, looking-glasses and the like for two huge areas of land. His intention was to be able to produce a document to prove the legality of the deal; and he was, in any case, one of the few to consider even token compensation necessary. Governor Bourke sent off a police magistrate to protect the Aborigines, armed with gifts for them of two hundred suits and five hundred red nightcaps. The magistrate, Lonsdale, set up a mission station near Melbourne and began to train a group of Aborigines as police, one of the many unsuccessful attempts made to use an Aboriginal disciplinary force to ensure the keeping of white law. Similarly unsuccessful was the founding of a school by the Church Missionary Society in 1837, since within two years all the children had fled. The Aboriginal population around Melbourne had declined from thousands to hundreds, mainly because of the extremely high infant mortality.

A realization of the seriousness of the situation prompted the proclamation of a New South Wales Aboriginal Protectorate Port Phillip District and the appointment of a Protector and four sub-protectors. Schools were built, food distribution centres established and attempts were made to teach agriculture. But the scheme failed, since the whites concerned were heavy-handed in their efforts to 'civilize the natives' and did not understand the cultural background and differing viewpoints of their charges. (The 1969 annual report of the Ministry for Aboriginal Affairs in Victoria indicated that the problem of bridging the cultural gap and motivating Aboriginal children to remain in school had not yet been solved.)[1] Furthermore the settlers complained that the best land was going 'to the blacks' who failed to develop it, though in fact increasingly large tracts were being made over to whites. Health problems became considerable, with a heavy toll from pneumonia and measles, alcohol and venereal disease and soon from malnutrition. A Committee of Inquiry was appointed by the New South Wales government in 1849 which, curiously enough, only sought evidence from white settlers north of the Murray. Not so curiously, it did not look for an Aboriginal viewpoint on the matter of their disposal at all, since this would have been completely contrary to the thinking of the time, which considered that Aborigines should be either exterminated or protected, treated as pests or as children, but certainly not consulted as sentient human beings. The Committee recommended termination of the protectorate, but the system continued after the establishment of Victoria as a self-governing State in 1851, albeit on a modified scale. By 1849 four ration depots had been set aside for the 'natives' in the Loddon Valley, the Goulburn Valley, the Western District and near Melbourne, which provided inadequate quantities of food, clothing and medicines. Soon assistance to Aborigines had become an occasional handout of blankets only; between 1852 and 1858, £11 10s. 1d. was the sum total spent on medical care.[2]

At the coming of the white man it was estimated that there were 11,500 Aborigines in Victoria. This number had fallen to 3,000 in 1851, to 1,700 in 1861, to 140 in 1915, and to 50 by 1921. Following a Select Committee of Inquiry in

1858, the Victorian colony established a Board for the Protection of Aborigines in 1860 and attempted to maintain a policy of control over education and of the provision of reserves, with rations for the old, the sick and the orphaned.

It was obvious by the 1860s that more protection was required for the remnants of the Aboriginal tribes and the churches were encouraged to open up reserves. Soon Anglican and Presbyterian–Moravian stations were caring for the Gippsland tribes, while the Aborigines along the Murray were left to camp on the properties of those settlers who would permit them to do so.

In 1869 an *Act to Provide for the Protection and Management of the Aboriginal Natives of Victoria* enabled regulations to be made regarding place of residence, terms of employment and care of Aboriginal children both for Aborigines of the full descent and part-Aborigines who habitually associated with Aborigines. By 1886 the definition of who was an Aborigine had been amended to include 'full-bloods, half-castes born before 1852, half-caste women married before 1887 to Aborigines and children of the above'. Whereas from 1860 to 1886 the main activity of the Protection Board had been to acquire reserves and encourage all Aboriginal people on to them, the policy changed from 1886 to 1924, the aim then being to move from the reserves all those part-Aborigines under thirty-four years of age capable of earning their living. Thus it was possible to close government stations in western and central Victoria, and to remove to Lake Tyers in eastern Gippsland some of those still needing support, and also Aborigines of the full descent. Under this forced assimilation policy, many children, as in New South Wales, were transferred to white institutions and rations were withdrawn from adults who resisted removal. During all this time (1886-1957) the Board had the authority to determine who was to live on the stations and to control them, while the powers given to station managers under the regulations gradually became more severe.

Southtown

Southtown, one of the two Victorian towns of our survey,
is situated in the Latrobe Valley, a wide plain running
through Gippsland on both sides of the Latrobe River. The
exploration of Gippsland was begun in May 1839 in a series
of journeys by Angus McMillan, who had on this and subsequent trips Aboriginal guides. It is thought likely that
originally there were a thousand Aborigines in Gippsland,
mostly centred on the lakes and along the rivers and sea
fringe. Food supplies and water were plentiful and there
was not the same need for itineracy as there was in the
hotter and drier parts of the country. Walter Firmin, one of
the early settlers, in a manuscript record states that though
Aborigines were numerous in the forest area near the present site of Southtown when the first whites arrived in
1844, there was none to be seen in 1874. Another settler,
Henry Mayrick, has left a graphic account of a 'black-
fellow' hunt in 1845 in which he declares his own inability
'to shoot blacks just for the fun of it', the implication being
that others had not his inhibition. As had happened in
New South Wales, when Aborigines discovered that their
previously plentiful supply of marsupials had dwindled as
a result of the settlers' clearing, sheep and cattle were
speared. One such episode occurred in the 1860s in Gippsland, as a result of which sixteen Aborigines were shot and
their bodies thrown into the Murrindal River at a place
known for many years afterwards as Slaughterhouse Gully.
It was not uncommon to see gun loopholes in the walls of
the log or slab huts attached to private cattle stations: a
state of seige against the Aborigines was commonly felt to
exist. Nevertheless, in Gippsland also, Aborigines proved
to be useful employees at wool-washing and other chores
for which they received rations and, in some instances, a
few shillings' pay.

The first Gippsland Aboriginal reserve was formed in
1859 by the Reverend F. A. Hagenauer, a Moravian Missionary, at Ramahyuck, fifteen miles from Sale, and comprised fourteen cottages, a meeting-house, church, school

and a boarding house where they were to be taught agriculture. An Anglican mission was established at Lake Tyers and by 1864 contained fifty Aborigines. In 1866 the Reverend John Bulmer, the missionary in charge, was already complaining that 'the tribes in Gippsland generally are very little inclined to help themselves in any way. I find a great difference between them and the Murray tribes' – an invidious comparison which is still being echoed today. By 1875, 4,200 acres of Crown land had been gazetted as Aboriginal reserve and in 1886 there were a hundred residents at Lake Tyers. After World War II there were few employment opportunities for the reserve's residents and living conditions were markedly below those of the general community. Mr Charles McLean, a former stipendiary magistrate, visited Lake Tyers during his 1956 investigation of the operation of the *Aborigines Act* 1928 and found thirty-three tiny cottages in a poor state of repair, with no running water or electricity and one communal bath-house for 209 residents. Wages were from £1 10s. 0d. ($3) to £3 ($6) per fortnight for adult males. From this time onwards the Aborigines Welfare Board came in for an increasing amount of criticism for its administration of Lake Tyers. After a visit there in July 1963, a delegation on behalf of the executive of the Melbourne Trades Hall Council stated that the Aboriginal residents had a 'deep resentment against the administration'. They were forced to 'live an undignified life', were 'treated like children', 'not allowed to look after themselves and, it is contended, cannot be trusted with money'. The Welfare Board's annual report for 1963 confirmed this assessment by stating that 'no real programme has been implemented to encourage independence ... because their life has been ordered for them and the residents have no training in making decisions for themselves'. It went on to state that the hand-out system of rations 'was a survival of an archaic scheme of benevolent protection', that there was almost complete segregation of the residents, who were dependent on the management and were given no realistic training for future employment. Reserves fitted Aborigines for living in reserves, and did not prepare them for life in the general community. They bred mutual antagonism between staff and inmates. Aborigines tended to blame white staff for all ills and were immobilized by hopeless resignation, knowing there was no redress. Regarded by whites as totally irresponsible, they were submitted to a degree of control usually reserved only for the mentally unfit.

Since many of today's Southtown Aboriginal residents come from a recent background of Lake Tyers and are there as a result of the Welfare Board's policy of resettling Aborigines from the reserve in the general community, it is important to bear its physical and emotional conditions in mind. Ingrained dependency is difficult to overthrow.

Brown coal was discovered in the Latrobe Valley in the early 1870s and in 1918 the State Electricity Commission was constituted for the purpose of co-ordinating the supply of electrical power throughout Victoria, with its headquarters a few miles from Southtown. In 1951 the Gas and Fuel Corporation established at Southtown a plant for the production of synthetic gas from brown coal briquettes. Today it is a more than ordinarily alive and varied town, with a population of 16,600, about one-quarter of whom are European migrants, attracted by the availability of employment and housing, Unfortunately, when questioning a cross-section of the townsfolk as to their attitudes to Aborigines (see Chapter 12), the sample was too small to differentiate migrant opinion from those of the Australian-born, particularly as many different nationalities and periods of residence in the town were represented. The main shopping centre reflects the cosmopolitan hinterland: the food shops are redolent with imported delicacies and wine sales almost equal those of beer.

Northtown

The upper reaches of the Murray River were discovered in 1824 and, by 1845, the surrounding land was almost completely occupied by pastoralists. Aborigines here resisted the acquisition of their lands more vigorously than the tribes in other regions of Victoria, but this only served to make their extinction quicker. G. A. Robinson, the Protector of Natives, in August 1846 found 'the natives well disposed' being 'regularly and usefully employed in Shepherding, Stockkeeping, bullock driving and domestic labour', though whites complained of attacks and there was sporadic shooting from the settlers.[3] Sturt reported a great reduction in the number of Aborigines he had seen along the river between his two visits of 1830 and 1838, a reduction which he attributed to the inroads of smallpox, measles, influenza, syphilis and also of shooting and poisoning. Indicative of the attitude of many of the settlers was an account by Peter Beveridge, who lived from 1845 to 1868 ten miles from Northtown and who was convinced that Aborigines were unable to distinguish between vice and virtue. 'Mercy being unknown, retribution was dealt out as only the brains of such bloodthirsty and ruthless savages could hatch.'[4] 'In the matter of arts and sciences they have not any', even the returning powers of the boomerang being a matter of accident. The Hon. A. F. A. Greeves recalls how after 'the blacks had been troublesome', they were hunted down by a group of whites. After one Aborigine had been shot through the head 'we cut off his left ear and carried it in my pocket as trophy of our success'.[5]

In 1879 two Aboriginal families took up land about ten miles from Northtown, one a part-Aborigine whose descendents now live in the town. By and large, however, the Aborigines who lived near the town in the early decades of this century left few descendants. Most of the present Northtown Aboriginal adults were born in New South Wales, Moulamein Reserve and Moonahcullah station.

With a total population of 7,400, Northtown regards itself as one of the leading towns in Victoria. Certainly, its tourist facilities are among the best; with a grand-scale outdoor folk museum, an old river-steamer converted into a restaurant, and a large amount of good accommodation, it is one of the holiday centres of the State, and basks in its reputation as an attractive and progressive city of particular interest to visit.

Notes

1. Charles Rowley has pointed out that for almost two centuries there has been an unsuccessful attempt to change Aborigines by education. He feels that even the use of special cross-cultural educational techniques are useless where the real barrier is Aboriginal resentment of inequality. (ROWLEY, C. D., *Aboriginal Policy and Practice*, vol. 3, *The Remote Aborigines*, Canberra, 1971, p. 351.)
2. Reported in BARWICK, DIANE, 'A Little More Than Kin', unpublished Ph.D. thesis, Australian National University, Canberra, 1963, p. 17.
3. STONE, A. C., 'The Aborigines of Lake Boga', Victoria, paper presented to Royal Society of Victoria, March 1911.
4. BEVERIDGE, PETER, *The Aborigines of Victoria and Riverina, as seen by Peter Beveridge*, Melbourne, 1889.
5. BROUGH SMYTH, R., *The Aborigines of Victoria*, Melbourne, 1878.

Chapter Eleven

Aborigines of Northtown and Southtown

The Household

The part-Aboriginal population of Southtown comprises 93 persons; just 0·6 per cent of the total population (see Table 5). Many of Southtown's Aboriginal families had only been in the town for four or five years, having been encouraged by the Aborigines Welfare Board to leave their former abode, Lake Tyers reserve, which the government planned in 1965 to close down gradually. (The plan was later reversed and the area declared to be an Aboriginal reserve, though those wishing to leave are still assisted by the Ministry of Aboriginal Affairs to do so, by housing grants and other means.) Northtown has 142 Aborigines, or 1·9 per cent of the total, a comparatively high ratio of Aborigines for a Victorian town. Social interaction among the Aboriginal Southtowners is almost exclusively in the Gippsland region; in fact, the rate of marriage within their own regional group among Gippslanders is the highest for any Aboriginal group in Victoria, at 49 per cent.[1] Although there is a white spouse in four of the fifteen 'Aboriginal' dwellings in Southtown, complaints about non-acceptance by the Southtown Aboriginal community came mostly from non-Gippsland Aboriginal spouses who were frequently made to feel outsiders.

Northtown's part-Aborigines are closely linked with those of other parts of the Mallee, by ties of kinship and association, but there are also ties with South Australia and the Cummeroogunja reserve in New South Wales. The Mallee as a whole has the lowest rate of marriage within its own area for all six of the Aboriginal country regions in Victoria. There is no sub-standard housing in North-

Table 5
Aboriginal Households, Southtown and Northtown

	Total Dwellings	Total Persons	Mean No. of persons per dwelling	% of total population	Occupancy Status %		Owner of Dwelling %			Housekeeping %		
					Own	Rent	MAA	HCV	Private	Good	Fair	Poor
Southtown	17	93*	5·5	0·6	5·9	94·1	29·4	58·8	11·8	40·0	33·3	26·7
Northtown	35	142†	4·0	1·9	0·0	100·0	39·3	21·4	39·3	‡	‡	‡

(*MAA* Ministry of Aboriginal Affairs; *HCV* Housing Commission of Victoria)

* This does not include sixteen itinerants located in Southtown at the time of the survey.

† In addition twenty-seven persons in four households living outside Northtown interacted almost exclusively with Northtown Aborigines and therefore formed part of the town community socially, though not geographically.

‡ Information not available.

town itself, although this still exists in the surrounding district.

Table 5 indicates a housing position which, on the face of it, is satisfactory, since the mean number of persons per dwelling for the whole of Southtown is 4·1 (Aboriginal 5·5) and for Northtown 3·8 (Aboriginal 4·0). However, this does not include the resident visitors who are an almost permanent feature of most Aboriginal households. The majority of Aborigines in both towns live in publicly-owned housing: 88 per cent in Southtown and 61 per cent in Northtown. This reflects the poor economic position of most families, who require to have their rent subsidized; and also an unwillingness on the part of white owners to let houses to Aborigines. At the time of the survey an Aboriginal couple had moved into Southtown so that the husband could take on a permanent job as gardener for a public utility. Their four children had had to be scattered with different relatives around Gippsland as they searched for a house. There was no overall shortage of accommodation, since skilled work had become increasingly hard to find, due to increase in automation, and a number of whites had recently moved out of the town. Dreading a refusal because of their racial origin, the couple had almost ceased to look, although they were longing to have their children with them. An officer from the local Ministry of Aboriginal Affairs began to assist them in their search. Several times when he had almost secured tenancy of a house which had been advertised, he was curtly shown the door on mentioning that he was acting on behalf of Aborigines. Housekeeping standards, which can be taken as one of the criteria of acculturation into the white society, are lower in Southtown than in the New South Wales town of Eastville (40 per cent 'good' as compared with 58 per cent), a not altogether surprising figure when it is realized that for the majority of families this is the first standard dwelling which they have occupied.

But mere statistics do not give a picture of an Aboriginal home. To the investigator it was a constant delight to visit an Aboriginal house which at any time of day would contain visitors, either dropping in for a chat, or staying for a week or more. Informality prevails, with people preparing meals for a segment of the household as they feel like it, comforting each other's children if they cry. Father, often unemployed, may be found at home, mending a broken toy, chatting with one of his mates who has just called in to exchange news. Homes which may lack the trim orderliness of the middle-class white have a vitality all their own. One such contained three generations, plus a cockatoo, and there were never fewer than ten people in the single, small livingroom. On one occasion, while the interviewer was trying to listen to grandpa's views, father was cooking some chops on the open fire, and the television set, around which several children were grouped, was on full-blast. Two babies crawled around the floor, taking swipes at whatever came their way and colliding horribly from time to time. The cockatoo screamed expletives, apparently its sole vocabulary. In the midst of this commotion, grandma sat down at the little hand-organ and began to sing hymns at the top of her voice, which she had learned 'at the Mission' in her youth. It was not surprising to hear that the white neighbours were not appreciative of the resultant uproar; and yet, a Ministry of Aboriginal Affairs officer remarked that, whenever she felt a bit dispirited, she would come and visit this family to be won back again to good cheer.

Education

In both Northtown and Southtown an Incentive Scholarship Scheme operated, designed to encourage better attendance and better performance in school by monetary payments to both parents and children, varying from $100 to $360 a year. The scheme was introduced in Northtown secondary schools in 1967 and in primary schools in 1968. In Southtown it commenced for both primary and secondary Aboriginal students in 1968. According to an evaluation published by the authors of the scheme,[2] a significant improvement in school attendance has resulted in the short time it has been in operation and, assuming that other variables have not intervened to influence attendance figures, it can be said to be successful. It is still too early to determine whether performance at school has also improved. The feelings of Aborigines toward the scheme (as with many other things) varied, and one must avoid the temptation to over-generalize. Many poor families who simply could not afford to keep their children in clothing and pocket-money at the standard of the general community were glad of the assistance. For the first time they had contact with a headmaster when they went to the school to collect their payments, and some rapport grew between the two different environments of school and home. On the other hand – and this applied particularly in Northtown – the special assistance, even while being accepted, was resented as being another aspect of white paternalism, a further example of the humiliation felt by Aborigines forced by circumstances to receive additional aid. The fact that the Incentive Scholarship Scheme had been well publicized in the local press in Northtown added to the fear of possible white resentment. Most teachers interviewed expressed some reservation as to the scheme. They pointed out that in various other countries, where this carrot method had been applied, it had been abandoned eventually for lack of result. One of them said of two Aboriginal children in her class:

Mary and Tom are sitting it out in the classroom because they've been told by their parents that they'll be punished if they don't. It's impossible to interest them in any aspect of school work, no matter what method I try. The only motivation they have is fear of a hiding; which keeps them coming, and even scraping 50 per cent in some subjects, but I'm sure they'll forget everything they've ever learned as soon as they leave here.

Another teacher expressed himself more strongly: 'What has payment got to do with personal fulfilment and love of learning? It's passing on to these kids one of the least attractive features of white society: its gross materialism.'

In Southtown seven Aboriginal children attended a High School opened in 1968, which had an experimental curriculum aimed at adaptation to the needs of each child. This school has become something of a star attraction for educators, both from within Victoria and from other States. Its main achievement is that the headmaster and staff see the parents as an important link in the educational process, and are always available to hear their views on such matters as curriculum content and disciplinary devices. The staff also make themselves available for informal private discussion with the students, who are encouraged to read and pursue learning on lines that are of particular interest to them. The library, which is in the centre of the school, is in constant use by eager learners, consulting books for information and for pleasure. As a result, the Aboriginal children attending this school indicated an unusual enthusiasm for learning and an eagerness to continue: a response to personalized tuition and relationships. Whether promise will give rise to performance remains to be seen: so far these seven children are distributed through the first three forms, while the two students attending technical school were in Forms 2 and 4 respectively. Several of the Aboriginal parents had been able to overcome their shyness sufficiently to discuss their children with the headmaster. One of them commented in mild surprise: 'He *listens* to you. He wants to know what you think about things. I had the feeling that he was real interested in Diane [her daughter].'

There is a mean retardation of eleven months among Northtown's secondary Aboriginal students and of sixteen and a half months in Southtown (see Table 6). There are no Aboriginal students above fourth form in either town. Of the total Aboriginal secondary enrolment in Southtown 89 per cent are in Forms I to III, and 75 per cent in Northtown. This contrasts with 68 per cent for the Victorian

Aborigines of Northtown and Southtown

Table 6

Secondary School Enrolments, Victoria, August 1969

Form	Northtown Ab. students as % of total Northtown Ab. enrolment N = 16	Southtown Ab. students as % of total Southtown Ab. enrolment N = 9	Victorian Ab. students as % of total Vic. Ab. enrolment* N = 243	Victorian students as % of total Victorian enrolment	Mean retardation of Northtown Ab. students N = 16 Years	Months	Mean retardation of Southtown Ab. students N = 9 Years	Months
I	31·2	33·3	40·2	23·8	–	9	1	1
II	31·2	22·2	29·7	23·4	–	7	1	3
III	12·5	33·3	18·2	21·0	1	4	–	10
IV	25·0	11·1	8·5	16·5	–	11	2	4
V	–	–	1·0	10·3	–	–	–	–
VI	–	–	0·8	4·9	–	–	–	–

* As at February 1967. Percentages do not total 100, since four children in Melbourne were in special forms which could not be categorized. (Data obtained from FELTON, P. E., 'Present Needs and Facilities – Victoria', in DUNN, S. S. and TATZ, C. M. (eds.), *Aborigines and Education*, Melbourne, 1969.)

community generally and is an indication, as in all other States, that the secondary school retention rate for Aborigines is low. The standard of formal education of the parent generation in both towns is also low, many being functionally illiterate and all unskilled, as is the case in so many Aboriginal communities because of the absence of educational facilities until comparatively recent years. And yet, educational and employment aspirations of both parents and children appeared relatively high. There has been a tendency to measure such aspirations by the middle-class standards of the officials dealing with Aborigines, rather than by those of white, unskilled workers. A recent study of a Melbourne working-class suburb[3] indicates that by and large 'older sons have followed in their father's footsteps and occupationally at least, we find little evidence that [working-class] parents have middle-class aspirations for their sons.' The authors go on to compare this situation with that in new American workers' housing areas, where new homes continue to shelter old, working-class values.

In another New South Wales study of Aborigines and whites,[4] matched for socio-economic status, it was the Aboriginal parents, living on a reserve, who showed higher educational aspirations for their children than did the whites in nearby urban areas; a significantly larger percentage wanting them to have technical or tertiary training. Aware of their intense deprivation, the adult reserve dwellers projected their aspirations on to the next generation, hoping that, by education, their children would enjoy a higher standard of living and have more opportunities than they themselves had experienced. However, among the Aboriginal children, the level of educational aspiration for both the reserve and the nearby town was slightly lower than for whites living in the same town or in a city close by. In Brisbane,[5] also, it has been found that Aboriginal mothers' aspirations for their children's education reflect a complete acceptance of the achievement orientation of the white society, especially of its middle class. The 'Newtown' (working-class) residents of white suburbia, on the other hand, found themselves housed in reasonable comfort at a standard similar to that of their neighbours, and could not view themselves or be viewed as unduly deprived.[6]

But the aspirations of Aboriginal children regarding employment possibilities were once again shown to be low in a survey of 122 Queenslanders, aged from 10 to 13 years.[7] Here, only seven aspired to the three top categories of occupation (on Congalton's seven-point scale) although the majority of both boys and girls looked to higher levels than those of their fathers. As with white children, the Aboriginal child's frame of reference extends no further than his family and friends and he therefore fails to consider high-status occupations as being attainable for himself, since he is aware of being a member of a low-status group, for whom opportunities have always been restricted.

It is obvious that, in order to raise children's aspirations and make them realizable, a preliminary step would have to be to raise the status of the whole Aboriginal community by giving them greater access to resources, both economic and technical.

The Ministry of Aboriginal Affairs, which was constituted at the beginning of 1968 under the provisions of the *Aboriginal Affairs Act* 1967, undertakes adult education classes at the Aboriginal Centre in Northtown. These deal not only with basic literacy and calculation skills, but also with civics courses concerned with how the general community operates. Interest in them, among a section of the Aboriginal population, has been considerable, although there have been grumblings from individuals that the wrong things were being taught at the wrong times.

There is no evidence that the advent of transistor radios and television into Aboriginal households has had a marked educational effect. Programmes favoured are those featuring popular singers, variety shows and Westerns, which undoubtedly bring glamour and excitement into drab lives (a function which makes them equally attractive to whites) and which may even have some broadening effect, albeit a spurious one. News and discussion items are often switched off, although a news commentary referring to Aborigines is followed with interest and relayed around the community, thus extending the feeling of separate identity to incorporate a wider group.

Employment

Employment opportunities are comparatively good in Southtown, as compared with the rest of Gippsland, since the State electricity authority alone employs 7,000 persons, many of whom are unskilled. Jobs are completely lacking, however, for juniors and females and no Aboriginal female was employed at the time of the survey. Though young Aboriginal people tend to leave school several classes higher than did their parents, this gives rise to no obvious advantage, as employment can only be found by travelling about Gippsland, staying with relatives here and there and picking up odd jobs, or going to Melbourne. Adolescents frequently move from household to household, establishing nomadic habits, which makes it difficult for them to settle at any one job later in life. Many older men have a lengthy background of intermittent work only, as a result of having lived at Lake Tyers or in parts of Gippsland where there is inadequate employment for the unskilled. At the time of the survey five of the fifteen households in Southtown were totally dependent on social service payments. Five males worked for the electricity authority and three on the railways, none was in private industry, though several were working on nearby farms on a temporary basis.

Attitudes to work are often casual, since to be unemployed carries no stigma in the Aboriginal community, nor does it appear to be questioned or resented by wives, who regard this state of affairs as at least intermittently inevitable.

There is a definite prejudice on the part of private employers against offering work to Aborigines, which is justified with the categorization: 'They're so unreliable.' It would appear that an employer who has had two or three Aborigines leave over a space of years is inclined to generalize as to Aboriginal shortcomings. The whites who leave in proportionately as great numbers and for no apparent reason are regarded as individuals, and their 'unreliability' is not, therefore, attributed to racial origin.

There is a deep-rooted conviction among Aborigines that they are bound to strike prejudice sooner or later on the part of management and workmates and that, in fact, most whites are tainted with the racist brush. Some feel almost impelled to live up to the white stereotype of Aboriginal unreliability. One middle-aged Aborigine, when asked his occupation, replied bitterly, 'I wander up and down the highway like you whitefellers expect me to.' There is a general reluctance to accept a job where no other Aborigines are employed, for fear of resultant loneliness. Whites have such different backgrounds and problems that it is difficult to make of them real confidants and friends. One of the factors contributing to job instability is recurrent illness or chronic ill-health: Aboriginal communities contain a disproportionate number of invalid pensioners, even among their younger members, and constantly poor diet does not add to working energy or efficiency. It was obvious that an accumulated sense of injustice sometimes impelled an Aborigine to refuse to appear at a workplace to which he had been sent by a government agency. One man commented:

They keep pushing us around all the time. My grandfather used to tell me about how they did the same to him. 'Go here, do this' is all we dark people ever hear. Why should I be expected to live like a white man and do as he says? I'll live my own life and my people will see to it that I don't starve.

There is no concrete proof to suggest that rate of job turnover in either of the two towns differs between Aboriginal and white unskilled workers. In fact, a survey of

Aboriginal employment, carried out by the Commonwealth Department of Labour and National Service in 1969 on an Australia-wide basis, gives evidence to show that retention rates for the same sort of jobs did not vary between white and Aborigine.

In Northtown difficulties in obtaining employment are even greater since, apart from the tourist and small manufacturing industries, there is only seasonal work for the unskilled, and none for juniors or females. Thirteen of Northtown's thirty-five households lived on social service benefits only, while the rest contained at least one employed person. Of these, fifteen were labourers and one a truck driver, two were painters, two were tourist guides, one was a liaison officer for the Ministry, and one a shearer.

In neither town were Aborigines employed in cafés and shops, which accords with the Australia-wide picture of the Aboriginal workforce. There is widespread disinclination to appoint Aborigines to jobs where they would have face-to-face contact with the public, except for the occasional opening in tourism.

A Commonwealth scheme which ensured payment while training for a skilled occupation was frequently brought to the attention of Aborigines in Northtown by the education officer employed at the time by the Ministry of Aboriginal Affairs and three people had begun training in sheep shearing, fashion modelling and as builder's apprentice respectively. The attitude of a certain section of the Aboriginal community was of interest in the scheme, and photographs and comments on the trainees in the local press were viewed with pride.

Health

As in New South Wales, the general standard of health for both towns is low. In Southtown commonest health problems include dietary inadequacies (in particular iron deficiency), recurrent respiratory infections, past history of tuberculosis, diabetes, and also premature ageing. Only three families were free from all these ailments. In Northtown chest and ear infections are prevalent, diet is inadequate and hygiene lacking. Even in the more acculturated families (that is, those who adhere to middle-class standards of household care, dress and behaviour) there is little realization of dietary values or the dangers of, for example, leaving a baby's feeding bottle exposed to flies. The reference group for behaviour in health, as in other matters, is the Aboriginal community. When being advised by a white doctor or nurse one can almost see the Aboriginal patient 'switching off', saying to him- or herself, 'This has nothing to do with me and the way our people have always acted.' In addition, doctors and nurses are often not consulted for fear of a mother being found at fault or inadequate by a white health official in the care of her family.

Women show a certain shyness in talking of birth-control and are often loathe to discuss contraceptive methods with a doctor who is both male and white. In Northtown the nursing sister employed by the Ministry of Aboriginal Affairs hesitated to broach the subject unless first approached by a patient, and this had only occurred once in her six months' employ. The advent of trained nurses in both towns, especially employed by the Ministry to attend to the health problems of Aboriginal families, was clearly having a beneficial effect. The nurses, by gradually building up a personal relationship with their patients, were increasingly able to function as health educators. They were also able to act as liaison officers between patients and other health personnel, while trying to avoid a situation of dependency on themselves. Most Aboriginal mothers were glad of their services and yet disliked the idea of the nurses only being available to Aborigines and not to the white community in need, a situation which they viewed as being very close to charity.

The New Zealand system might well serve as model here, whereby visiting District Public Health nurses pay home visits to all patients in a given area who are in need.

They are employed by the Health Department and not by the Department of Maori Affairs although, in the event, they have a disproportionate number of Maoris among their clientele, since the latter are likely to be poorer, worse housed and worse fed than their white neighbours. Nurses who are Health Department employees have the advantage of more possibilities of promotion, in-service training, and access to the many facilities which a Health Department provides. They can also offer special inducements to Aborigines to train as nurses and nursing aides by offering scholarships and lowering entry qualifications if need be.

Attitude to Institutions for Aborigines

As has been mentioned, most of Southtown's adult Aborigines have a background either of institutionalization at Lake Tyers, where responsibility was not required of them, or of a semi-nomadic life through east Gippsland in search of work or sustenance. In either case their personal history is one of substandard housing, great poverty and little education. It is not surprising therefore to find that their self-image is one of an embattled minority, opposed by the white community in general and in particular by its Aboriginal institutions. Though appreciation was often expressed of individual staff members of the Ministry of Aboriginal Affairs, there was deep resentment of the Ministry as such which, at the time of the survey, had just finished building an Aboriginal Centre in the town. There were many complaints that the local Aboriginal community had not been consulted as to its requirements, which were primarily for a hall as a district meeting place. (The Ministry's emphasis at the Centre was to be on youth education and training in household care.) Even the naming of the Centre was by decision of the Ministry. On the other hand there was a certain pride in the fact that a substantial and expensive building in the centre of town should have the word 'Aboriginal' attached.

The Ministry of Aboriginal Affairs in Victoria has been divided into administrative regions, each in charge of a social worker. These white professionals, not surprisingly, are seen by their Aboriginal clients to identify with and to be agents of the middle class. The black psychologist, Kenneth Clark, has pointed out that 'it is hard for many of them [social workers] to understand why they are irrelevant to the root problems of the poor.'[8] Their concern is to help the client 'adjust' to the circumstances of his life, not to change those circumstances; to concentrate on the strengths and weaknesses of the individual, not the injustices with which he is beset. Paulo Freire, the famous South American educator, expresses a similar viewpoint: welfare recipients are treated as marginal men who deviate from the general configuration of a 'good, organized and just society'.[9] (Freire, in practice, inclines to listen to and learn from, rather than to counsel, members of under-privileged communities, assisting them to organize for social action to secure what they believe to be their rights.)

Aborigines in Victoria have not the organization or power for collective decision-making and are loathe to submit to counselling on an individual basis, since this implies concurrence with the interests and values of the major society. Frequently, Aboriginal deviance is a mute protest at being frozen out of the decision-making process and the lack of ability to fulfil their own basic needs. The 'assistance' obtained from the social workers is regarded as a manipulative device to reinforce a racist and oppressive social system, since it is not forthcoming to formulate group grievances and then attempt collective solutions to problems. In many instances there is an assumption on the part of the social worker that the values of his society (in which he himself has been socialized and which have served him satisfactorily) are absolute values to which the client must be cajoled to conform: such as the need to achieve, respect for authority, the importance of planning ahead, and of security. Clients who deviate from these norms are dubbed beyond the pale of help and are reluctantly abandoned.[10]

Counselling techniques conducted on an individual basis tend to become concentrated on problems of psychological adjustment, whereas the Aboriginal client does not believe that he can afford to indulge in neuroses or nervous tensions; his problems are more fundamental and are usually caused by social deprivation – chiefly lack of money: no house, no food, no medical attention and no power to acquire these essentials. And so the gulf remains between administrators and those administered, with continuing frustration on both sides.

A somewhat similar attitude was evinced towards the Aborigines' Advancement League (Victoria), one of the leading Aboriginal voluntary agencies. The resentment was two-fold. The League was at the time of the survey dominated by whites and had been influenced by a small group of ex-Cummeroogunja Aborigines, who had ignored the needs of the people of Gippsland. The fact that Gippslanders are low in the esteem of Victorian Aborigines of other regions has previously been observed.[11]

Northtown's view of its Aboriginal Centre, opened in 1967, was less stringent. The Centre was in daily use as a meeting place and focal point for adult education, craft classes, gatherings of the Aboriginal Assembly (whose meetings all adult members of the Northtown community were free to attend) and a sewing circle. Once weekly it was also used for pre-school sessions run by Monash University in conjunction with the Ministry. Here again there was resentment of authority and regret that control of the Centre was not in Aboriginal hands and was not used sufficiently in the evenings or at the weekend. Feelings toward the local Aboriginal Affairs Committee, inaugurated in July 1966, had varied over the two years of its existence, depending on changing personnel and the degree to which they were prepared to do battle on the Aboriginal behalf. At the time of the survey the Committee was serving the role of ombudsman through whom appeal could be made to governmental authority.

Aboriginal Culture

Some traces of the traditional culture remain in both towns in a knowledge of a few words or phrases of the vernacular, and in medical remedies still used by the older people. The medicinal properties of goanna oil, and of 'old man's weed' (only obtainable from a particular locality) are still subscribed to as cures for boils, colds and pain. Though these are usually jealously guarded from whites, there was a partly favourable response to the suggestion in Southtown that they be published in a type of 'recipe book' that would be a uniquely Aboriginal contribution to the general society. The word *Kuri* is used to denote Aborigine (now often spelled *Koorie*) and *gaba* (which has now degenerated to *gubs*) for whites. 'Dark people' is still used, but 'Aborigines' is becoming commoner among the young. Positive distaste was expressed for 'blacks' as being derogatory and inaccurate though, since the time of the survey, the word has come into limited currency among the young and radical.

The 'hairy men' of tradition with whom recalcitrant children used to be threatened are still invoked among the Gippslanders and ex-Cummeroogunja inhabitants, though their effectiveness as a threat to the young is dwindling.

Attitudes to White Society

The American social scientist, Hyman Rodman, has formulated the concept of the 'lower-class value stretch', an adaptive mechanism by which

the lower class person, without abandoning the general values of the society, develops an alternative set of values ... [so that such people have] ... a wider range of values than others within the society. They share the general values of the society ... but in addition they have stretched these values or developed alternative values, which help them to adjust to their deprived circumstances.[12]

141

They are not ignorant of or indifferent to conventional norms and values, but realize that it would be foolish and perpetually frustrating to maintain full allegiance to conventional norms when it is obvious that they will be unable to achieve satisfactorily in those terms. The Aboriginal families of Southtown are aware that they are expected to work regularly, marry legally and be clean and industrious, and often express approval of this type of behaviour. Families notorious for alcoholism and light-fingeredness are the first to profess allegiance to the Protestant ethic: no doubt a prime example of 'value stretch'. A linguist working in the Aboriginal field has observed: 'It is curious how much of white–Aboriginal discourse centres around responsibilities as opposed to an alternative focusing on achievement.'[13] He goes on to state that Aboriginal women 'could be made to respond almost at the push of a discourse button about the necessities of having fed the baby, cleaned the house, cooked the food, etc.' There is a constant pressure by the general community towards the realization and not just the espousal of these ideals; and in particular, by the Ministry of Aboriginal Affairs, which gives a $1,500 gift deposit for a house to those likely to keep up the payments. Operating side by side with these 'push' factors from the white community and the normal desire to conform to social mores, the 'pull' factors continue: non- or grudging acceptance by whites; the reassurance of belonging to the Gippsland Aboriginal community, with its fellowship and financial support (even though this can no longer be relied on under any circumstances); the strong sense of group identity and of a shared history.

In Northtown the Aboriginal community was dichotomized between an 'upper' group, conforming to social standards and a 'lower' group which rejected those standards, thereby making itself unacceptable to the rest of the Aboriginal as well as to the general community. As further services and assistance, particularly in education, are becoming available through Federal and State government sources, the rift between the two sections is likely to become greater and the rejection of the less successful stronger. This stratification of what has been until recently an undiversified community is beginning to emerge in Southtown and has been carried to a further point in Northtown. This is by no means a new phenomenon, but was observed as long ago as the 1940s in Moree, New South Wales, which had two clearly defined classes in the Aboriginal community;[14] and since that time has been found in numerous other Aboriginal groups.

The more thoughtful members of Northtown's 'middle-class' Aboriginal community were uneasy at this trend, which they considered had been reinforced by conferences of FCAATSI, which were dominated by the more successful, whose aims might be totally divergent from the rest. Another Northtown Aborigine saw the only hope of obtaining independence for the weaker section was to provide a sheltered workshop, suitable for those with no previous experience of steady employment, where the pleasures of companionship would induce a gradually increasing adherence to the value of work.

The boredom and bewilderment observed by Diane Barwick[15] among Melbourne Aborigines when education and employment were introduced as conversational topics no longer applies to the upper Northtown group, to whom upward social mobility has become a goal. Information on job and scholarship opportunities for their children is sought and passed on. Yet, even among this section, 'going level' is still prized: those who rise too far and too fast both socially and economically risk losing close membership of their own extended kinship group.

Alcoholism and the Law

The addiction to alcohol with which Aborigines are attributed by the white community is not entirely a figment of the imagination. About half the Aboriginal families in both towns contain at least one person whose drinking is so heavy that it interferes with regular employment. In Southtown much of the heavy drinking is done by itinerants, closely related to the householder with whom they periodically stay, a number of whom are always to be found in the town (as previously mentioned, there were sixteen such at the time of the survey). In both towns alcoholics tend to gather at a central point, where they are readily seen and heard. Police confirm that disturbances occur on these occasions among Aborigines and not between Aborigines and whites and that, as in New South Wales, it is a minority of the Aboriginal community who appear time and again as offenders.

Tobin[16] and others have suggested that there is little stigma for Aborigines in going to prison since, like the blacks in the United States, they consider themselves as hostages in the race war and regard periodic convictions as inevitable. Eggleston[17] has refuted the suggestion, indicating that her interviews with Aboriginal prisoners disclosed that they all vehemently disliked gaol and were apt to suffer later on from the effects of stigmatization as criminals. These two seemingly opposite views could be reconciled by acknowledging that Aborigines, like almost anyone else, dislike the restrictions and indignities of prison life, and find it hard to adjust to the outside community after a period of institutionalization; while being labelled a 'criminal' makes them even more prone to discrimination than before. On the other hand, if they are regarded as unlucky rather than at fault by their own community, a gaol sentence will not bring in its train feelings of shame or guilt (unless they are scorned as lowering the prestige of all Aborigines by having publicly 'made a nuisance of themselves').

It is worth recalling that alcoholism is also rife in the white community, although it is not nearly so visible. More than half the admissions to Pentridge gaol in Melbourne are connected with alcoholism; while the Sydney coroner recently stated that there was a drink factor in no less than 70 per cent of inquests.[18]

With Aborigines, where drinking occurs, it often forms part of a syndrome or behavioural pattern which has developed as an adjustment to the stresses occasioned by the deculturation or acculturation process of recent Aboriginal history. Alcoholism is frequently a cover for aggression; negative sanctions being only lightly imposed by society for aggression committed while in a state of intoxication. The pattern of drinking is not racially determined, since there is no evidence that the Aborigine is inherently more susceptible to alcoholism. The causes must be sought in historical, social and cultural factors. A 'deep sense of inadequacy and inferiority, growing from his relations with the white man', is seen as the most important factor tending towards heavy drinking among the culturally marginal.[19] It has also been pointed out that 'permissiveness to heavy drinking seems most often found in the lower socioeconomic strata' and that for such people, drunkenness on a Saturday evening tends to be socially acceptable.[20]

Table 7

Southtown and District Aboriginal Charges, 1965 and 1966

	Total No. of Aboriginal Charges	Drunk and Disorderly	
		No.	%
1965	97	86	88·6
1966	114	69	60·5

(Total Aboriginal population of Southtown police district is unknown.)

Table 7 gives the 1965 and 1966 figures for Aboriginal charges in Southtown and district. Precise figures for subsequent years were not available, though there was evidence to indicate that the total number of Aboriginal charges had increased and the percentage of drunk and disorderly charges had further declined. Numbers of Aborigines in the area fluctuate considerably, but it is unlikely that there has been a substantial overall increase. The drunk and disorderly charges include fewer than twenty men (most not permanent residents of the town but related to town families) who come up repeatedly on the same charge and who are sentenced to seven days' imprisonment on each occasion. Police complained that there was no men's home or treatment centre to which such people could be referred.

Northtown's charge figures for the six months ending 19 September 1969 are given in Table 8. All save one of these charges (that concerning car-tampering) were connected with alcohol. A similar pattern has been found to exist in Western Australian country towns, although not on so marked a scale: 83 per cent of all charges against Aborigines in 1966 were for drunkenness.[21]

Table 8

Northtown and District Aboriginal Charges, Six Months
Ending 19 September 1969

Charge	No.
Drunk and disorderly	29
Insufficient lawful means of support	5
Assault by kicking	1
Indecent language	2
Unlawful assault (domestic)	1
Tampering with motor-car	1
Total	39

(Total Aboriginal population of Northtown police district is unknown.)

Attitudes towards the police and legal processes in general were uniformly negative. The law was seen as the punitive arm of white society, always poised ready to strike, never as an instrument of justice which could be used by black and white alike. Perusal of the files of the Social Welfare Department of Victoria supports this contention.[22] It is very rare for Aboriginal parents in dire straits who are unable to care for their children to take them to the police for protection, as frequently happens with white parents similarly placed. They are almost invariably left with relatives, any action to take them into State care being initiated by the police.

Recent Historical Factors

It is not possible to appreciate the tentative approach of Aborigines of both towns without considering events of recent history.

In May 1965 the Aborigines Welfare Board announced a plan to build a transit village in Southtown, to be used as a training centre for about ten years, and to close the reserve at Lake Tyers. This village was to consist of three or four family homes, two or three units for elderly couples and three or four units for single people. At this time five Aboriginal families were living in different areas of the town. The Southtown Shire Council was approached to rezone four and a half acres of agricultural land as a residential area. On 6 May the Council passed a resolution agreeing 'with the assimilation of two or three families of aborigines [sic] but does not agree with the Aborigines Welfare Board's proposal to establish a settlement at Southtown.' By September 1965 a protest committee had been formed in Southtown, since there was widespread objection to the transit village. By 28 October the Minister for Housing and Aboriginal Affairs stated that the idea would be shelved and that 'local opposition to the settlement plan was the determining factor' in the shelving. A meeting of the Council on 16 November 1966 expressed concern, none the less, at 'the increasing numbers of Aborigines occupying homes in this municipality' and their overcrowding; to which the Board replied on 12 December 1966 in conciliatory vein: 'It is possible that one or two houses owned by the Aborigines Welfare Board in South-town may have to be left unoccupied till suitable families are available.' In February 1968 the new Ministry of Aboriginal Affairs requested a building permit from the Council to provide a hostel for six to eight boys aged sixteen to twenty-five years, who would be under the supervision of a married couple. Since the scheme involved limited numbers and limited time of occupation, permission was granted for a Centre which was to house Ministry staff and have two houses attached for training in household care: again, its occupants would be transitory and supervised.

A not dissimilar situation had arisen in Northtown where, by 1951, a grossly sub-standard Aboriginal shanty settlement of thirty-one persons, twenty-one of whom were children, had grown up by the Murray river, just on the outskirts of Northtown. Many had come from Balranald mission in search of independence and work. A local sergeant of police, together with a voluntary committee, constructed a Native Children's Recreation Centre across the river in New South Wales, which was opened in December 1952, and consisted of a recreation room, dormitory and bath-house, all situated near the parents' huts. By 1959 about a hundred Aborigines had settled in the district. The following year, four cottages had been supplied near the river and one family had been placed in standard housing in the town. Until 1969 the settlement served as a staging camp, most of Northtown's present residents having passed through it before establishing themselves in the town. The remaining cottages were demolished in mid-1969 since they were considered to be a perpetuation of sub-standard housing. Aborigines pointed out, however, that no alternative provision had been made for newcomers to the town, without resources of any kind, to house their families while seeking employment. On 17 June 1967 the Melbourne *Age* reported that there were five hundred Aborigines living in tents, huts and humpies along the Murray River, in the vicinity of Northtown. This was in addition to the ten families in the town living in Housing Commission or Aborigines Welfare Board houses. On 19 June the Minister for Housing and Aboriginal Affairs announced that fifteen houses would be built for Aborigines in Northtown. Immediately unease was displayed and protests registered on the basis that these (Housing Commission) homes should be available to whites; that many Aborigines were not yet ready for occupation of standard housing; that they 'should not be taken away from a primitive way of life and massed together'; and that already forty to fifty additional Aboriginal families had arrived in Northtown from as far afield as the Northern Territory and Queensland at the prospect of improved conditions.[23]

The 'mass' housing scheme was dropped, but the Aborigines Welfare Board acceded to requests of the local Aboriginal Affairs Committee to buy and renovate an old building in a prominent position in the town for use as an Aboriginal centre. This was opened in October 1967 and an adult education officer appointed in February 1968.

In recent years, in three of our four towns, the possibility of a group of Aborigines settling together in the town has been seen as a threat by the white townspeople, thus demonstrating latent fear and resentment to Aborigines as a group. Aborigines are, on their side, acutely aware of the feeling against them, despite protestations of friendship from individuals. The two-fold result of such displays of antagonism has been a steady Aboriginal wariness towards intrusion into the major society and its institutions, and a strengthening of group cohesion.

Aborigines of the two Victorian towns, like the two in New South Wales, were notable for their absence from service clubs, parent committees and all other voluntary organizations. Their absence was noticeable also in calls on community services (ranging from the emergency housekeeper scheme to the library) though the policy of the Ministry of Aboriginal Affairs is towards utilization of general services rather than provision of specialized ones.

Words or Blows

At the suggestion of the Adult Education Officer in North-town two Aborigines had joined a men's lodge and one woman had become a member of the Country Women's Association. It was still too early to judge whether this membership would be lasting or meaningful.

Notes

1. LIPPMANN, LORNA, 'A Statistical Analysis of the Victorian Part-Aboriginal Population', unpublished MS., Centre for Research into Aboriginal Affairs, Melbourne, 1969.

2. BOAS, P. and MUNDAY, J., *Aboriginal Education Incentive Scholarship Fund*, mimeographed, 1969.

3. BRYSON, LOIS and THOMPSON, FAITH, *An Australian Newtown: Life and Leadership in a Working-Class Suburb*, Melbourne, 1972, p. 42.

4. CLARK, HELEN M., 'Aboriginal Assimilation in Two Communities', M.Sc. thesis, University of Newcastle, 1971.

5. BIDDLE, ELLEN H., 'The Assimilation of Aborigines in Brisbane 1965', Ph.D. thesis, University of Missouri.

6. BRYSON, LOIS and THOMPSON, FAITH, op. cit.

7. GOUGH, I. R., 'Aspirations of Aboriginal Children', *Australian Psychiatrist*, vol. 5, no. 3, November 1970, pp. 267–9.

8. CLARK, KENNETH B., 'The Psychology of the Ghetto', in ROSE, PETER I. (ed.), *The Study of Sociology*, New York, 1970, p. 483.

9. FREIRE, PAULO, *Pedagogy of the Oppressed*, New York, 1968, p. 60.

10. The main arguments in the foregoing have been derived from HOROWITZ, I. S. and LIEBOWITZ M., 'Social Deviance and Political Marginality: Toward a Redefinition of the Relation between Sociology and Politics', *Social Problems*, vol. 15, 1968, pp. 280–96; and PEMBERTON, A. G. and LOCKE, R. G., 'Towards a Radical Critique of Social Work and Welfare Ideology', *Australian Journal of Social Issues*, vol. 6, no. 2, 1971, pp. 95–105. An increasing number of writers support these contentions.

11. BARWICK, DIANE E., 'The Self-Conscious People of Melbourne', in REAY, MARIE (ed.), *Aborigines Now*, Sydney, 1964.
12. RODMAN, HYMAN, 'The Lower-Class Value Stretch', *Social Forces*, December 1963.
13. JERNUDD, BJOERN H., 'Social Change and Aboriginal Speech Variation in Australia', in *Working Papers in Linguistics*, Honolulu, University of Hawaii, no. 4, May 1969.
14. REAY, MARIE, 'A Half-Caste Community in North-Western New South Wales', *Oceania*, vol. 15, pp. 296–323.
15. BARWICK, DIANE E., 1963. 'A Little More than Kin', unpublished Ph.D. thesis, Australian National University, Canberra, 1963.
16. TOBIN, PETER, 'Aborigines and the Political System', in STEVENS, FRANK S. (ed.), *Racism: The Australian Experience*, vol. 2, *Black Versus White*, Sydney, 1972, p. 72.
17. EGGLESTON, ELIZABETH, 'Aborigines and the Administration of Justice', unpublished Ph.D. thesis, Monash University, 1970.
18. Figures quoted by DAX, E. CUNNINGHAM, *The Problem of Alcoholism and Its Treatment*, paper presented to Institute of Social Welfare, May 1970. Surveys indicate that 5 per cent of males and 1 per cent of females in the general population are likely to have severe drinking problems.
19. DOZIER, E. P., 'Problem Drinking among American Indians: The Role of Socio-Cultural Deprivation', *Quarterly Journal of Studies on Alcohol*, vol. 27, p. 85.
20. SARGENT, M. J., 'Heavy Drinking and its Relation to Alcoholism', *Australian and New Zealand Journal of Sociology*, vol. 4, no. 2, October 1968.
21. EGGLESTON, E., op. cit., p. 13.
22. By kind permission of the Minister for Social Welfare, Victoria.
23. Representations made by a deputation from Northtown City Council to the Premier of Victoria, as reported in the *Age* and the *Herald*, 23 June 1967.

Chapter Twelve

White Racial Attitudes

Only a person of courage (or could it be foolhardiness?) would attempt to quantify racial attitudes as they are expressed in day-to-day conversation. Here is an Eastville factory operative, adding a few heart-felt comments to the questionnaire which he had just completed:

Some of the Abos in this town make you sick. Sitting around, whingeing all day, cadging a few bob here and there, not prepared to do a fair day's work. Mind you, some of these fellers try hard to get work and they get passed over all the time by the bosses, who just don't like blackfellers. The government should help them more, but they're too busy fighting Yankee wars in Vietnam. Why don't they let those little yeller fellers fight it out for themselves? Why should us Aussies have to die for them? My kids ask me about this here Abo problem and I tell them it's always been like that: whites lording it over blacks, not giving them a fair go. Took over their country, we did, and give them nothing in return. I heard one of them experts on TV the other night and he reckoned Abos have got as much brains as anyone. Myself, I don't think they have, not the types you see around here, anyway. Of course, the trouble with some of these coloured johnnies is they got *too* much brain and chisel us Aussies out of jobs. Take the Chinks, for instance. Crawled in here in the early days and here they stay – never mind whose bread they take. But you aren't allowed now to say you don't like coloureds. All them brains on TV and in the papers they say you've gotta give them a fair go. But *they* don't have to be at the factory at eight every morning, rain, hail or shine and then home for tea and a bit of telly and then hit the sack and to work again. And what for? To pay taxes to keep some fat Abo sitting on his arse. But I reckon they aren't all like that. There's an Abo who works with me in the factory. It was thanks to me he got the job. Put in a good word for him with the boss, I did. Now we're mates. We swap yarns and eat our tucker together at dinner-time. I reckon there's a lot of Abos like this bloke. Not much schooling – but they know a lot. They get their clever way of thinking from their parents and grandparents before them. They was a clever lot, the way they thought up the boomerang and managed to keep themselves in tucker when there weren't much about.

Feelings of resentment loom up about coloured people, about bosses, about the government, whenever this man talks. Yet it is all interlarded with a practical kindliness and even admiration of the people he intermittently despises. His life is insecure, his emotions complex. The resentment at his own lack of recognition wells up against the rich and the ne'er-do-well alike. Confusion turns to hate and hate is more easily directed at people in the vicinity who are highly visible than it is upon a whole social and economic system and those whom it favours.

What, in essence, is an attitude? The social psychologists have propounded numerous definitions, but one which is generally acceptable is: 'The tendency to evaluate an object or the symbol of that object in a certain way.'[1]

In order to elicit attitudes towards Aborigines, a questionnaire (see Appendix I) was administered to a cross-section of the white population in each town. Sometimes this was followed by free-flowing monologue. A few interviewees sought out the interviewer at a later stage to continue the discussion; others were so little interested that they showed impatience at being questioned at all.

Aboriginal opinion had been almost unanimous that Eastville, though only twenty miles distant, was less tolerant towards Aborigines than was Westville. A number of white officials concurred in this view, yet perusal of the 1966 census statistics reveals two similarly structured white communities in the two towns as far as most of the variables likely to affect race relations are concerned, Westville in fact having a higher ratio of Aborigines to whites, while educational, employment and age levels are about evenly matched (see Table 9).

Table 9

Structure of General Population, Eastville and Westville (in percentages)

	Population under 40	Born in Aust.	Employees in total workforce	Unemployed	Primary schooling only	Aborigines in total population
Eastville (N=18,600)	67·3	95·3	82·3	2·5	38·3	0·8
Westville (N=8,200)	66·6	96·8	84·0	1·9	41·4	1·5

There was not as great a difference in the empirical appraisal of racial attitudes in the Victorian towns, though there was general concensus that Northtown was fairly tolerant to Aborigines and Southtown less so, though improving.

In order to obtain a representative sample from each community, the households were chosen by selection of dwellings by random numbers from a complete list supplied by the local authorities. Each house was visited by a trained interviewer who asked for the male householder or his wife, alternating between the two. Refusal rate was low at 4 per cent in Eastville and Northtown, 2 per cent for Westville and Southtown. This did not necessarily imply concurrence with the aims of the survey, or a high level of interest in the topic. A variety of factors were at work to encourage compliance: many wives were glad of company to liven up the day's routine; husbands were glad of a break in their gardening chores; both were flattered at having their opinions sought; and the innate courtesy of the country-dweller to a stranger ensured co-operation.

At the same time as the questionnaire, a social-distance scale, a variant of the Bogardus Scale, was also administered[2] (Appendix II). The concept of social distance helps evaluate the extent of discrimination and to delineate it as a continuum. As Park[3] expressed it: 'Everyone, it seems is capable of getting on with everyone else provided each preserves his proper distance.' Social distance, in fact, is the degree of closeness of association to which an individual is willing to admit members of another group. The expression of this distance is determined by a combination of individual sentiment and shared norms as to what constitutes proper behaviour in a particular society and can reflect either negative attitudes or a feeling of cultural distance (a relative lack of common interests or experiences). Numerous American experiments suggest that verbal responses to social-distance scales may be poor predictors of actual behaviour, since feelings of social distance towards an out-group may be influenced by such factors as dislike of the out-group, the inappropriateness of the situation, fear of the anticipated reactions of the in-group, fear of the responses of the out-group or shyness regarding unfamiliar social situations.

For example, coloured people coming to a manager of an hotel as potential guests have been accepted, even though the manager had just been expressing his views against blacks with great vehemence. In the event, his feelings were not strong enough to overcome his embarrassment at looking two pleasant, courteous people in the eye and telling them they were not wanted. An ugly scene might have ensued, resulting in the manager's loss of face; or the coloured guests may have been accompanied by a white man, a friend or customer of the manager; or the latter may have calculated that cash was more important than dislike. Similarly, a manager who professes ideals of the brotherhood of man may reject black guests, 'because they would drive white customers away'.

The feeling of social distance is usually greater for close or primary than for secondary social contacts; while acceptance in a relationship of marriage is the most convincing sign of all of real social acceptance and is a necessary potential for successful social mobility. The scale measures the degree of social distance that the respondent wishes to keep between himself and members of three out-groups: Aborigines, part-Aborigines and Italians. (Italians were chosen for purposes of comparison with attitudes to Aborigines since they are the largest migrant group, and an easily identifiable one.) The respondent was asked to indicate to which categories he would admit members of the out-group as relative by marriage', 'as a family friend' and so on.

Respondents were also asked personal details which might be relevant to attitudes, such as age, occupation, education, length of residence in the town and amount of contact with Aboriginal people.

Measurement of Attitudes to Aborigines

An attitude scale was compiled from answers to four of the questions which were most revealing of personal bias. These were:

Question 2. What, in your view are the main disadvantages (if any) under which Aborigines live at present in .... [your town]?

Question 4. How do you think Aborigines would respond to these improvements [by the government to Aboriginal conditions]?

Question 7. Could Aborigines do more to help themselves? If so, what?

Question 10. Given the same opportunities, could Aborigines do as well as whites?

A panel of three independent judges allotted a score varying from 0 to 2 for each answer, the highest scorers being those with the most favourable attitudes, the maximum score being 8 (see Table 10). Respondents whose attitudes were adjudged most favourable were those who considered Aboriginal disadvantages to be of an environmentally determined rather than of an inherent kind (Question 2); that Aborigines would respond well to government-inspired improvements in the situation (Question 4); that Aboriginal inequalities were not primarily self-imposed (Question 7); and that Aboriginal ability equalled that of whites (Question 10).

Those who were favourable came forth with such comments as:

How can they be expected to pull themselves up by the bootstraps, when they haven't any boots?

It's hard enough for whites to get cheap housing in this town. Must be impossible for the dark folk.

The government *should* do more for them. After all, it was their country ... but I've never stopped to think just what.

Anybody would respond to a bit of kindness and practical help. After all, they're only human.

Those who can get jobs and look after their own families, do so. But if they can't, it's almost impossible for any family, black or white, to live on Social Welfare.

Of course, Aborigines do as well as whites if they get a fair go, but mostly they don't *get* a fair go.

Those who were unfavourable made such remarks as:

They're their own worst enemies. If they'd just get off the booze and do a bit of work for a change ...

The government's always pouring the taxpayer's money down the drain on that lot. But what's the good? They *will* go walk-about – it's in the blood.

They'll never do as well as whites. Haven't got the brains, and anyway, they're just bone lazy.

157

Table 10
Attitude Scale (Judges' Ratings)

Score	Westville (N=50)		Eastville (N=50)		Southtown (N=50)		Northtown (N=50)	
	M	F	M	F	M	F	M	F
8	0	0	0	0	0	1	0	0
7	1	0	1	0	0	0	0	2
6	0	5	5	4	3	2	3	1
5	11	9	6	7	4	2	7	5
4	7	8	5	7	7	6	5	7
3	4	2	5	6	6	8	7	3
2	1	0	1	1	3	3	2	5
1	1	1	2	0	2	1	1	2
0	0	0	0	0	0	2	0	1
Favourable (5–8)	26		23		12		18	

Those respondents whose score was five or more, about 40 per cent in all, were considered to have favourable attitudes. On this basis the number of whites with favourable attitudes in Eastville – the town of worst repute of the four for race relations – is smaller than in Westville. The difference is not statistically significant but is greater than in the Victorian towns. This may reflect the fact that a sympathetic group in Eastville (and a more persistent one in Westville) have taken up the civil rights cudgels on the Aboriginal behalf and have brought before the public the positive aspects of Aboriginal life, with exhibitions of traditional arts and crafts, lectures on the Aboriginal situation and the like. It is not surprising that the smallest number of 'favourable' persons is found in Southtown where there is the widest gap between the value systems of the Aboriginal and white populations. The attitudes towards Aborigines of 60 per cent of all interviewees varied from the mildly to the very unfavourable.

There is little difference between the scores of males and females in each town, though females on the whole tend to be less favourable. This is in accord with the findings of many other race relations studies which have shown women generally to express less favourable attitudes, since many are dependent on men for social status and feel that they are in too vulnerable a position to be other than conformist. Williams,[4] on the other hand, found prejudice to be slightly higher in some instances among males, in others among females, indicating that other variables such as amount and type of contact have entered to complicate the picture.

Relationship Between Attitude and Background Factors

A five-point favourability scale was compiled from the scores in Table 9 and related to personal data recorded for each respondent. It can be seen in Table 11 that the 6 per cent whose overall attitudes were very unfavourable (that is, who scored 0 to 1) had little or no contact with Aborigines. No better indication could be given of the social separation of white and Aboriginal communities than the fact that no respondent in any of the four towns had had a 'great deal' of contact with Aborigines, despite the fact that a number lived in the same street and attended the same workplace as an Aborigine and had done so for a considerable period. Only 13 per cent had had a 'fair amount' of contact, while about half had had no contact at all.

There would appear to be little association between favourable attitudes to Aborigines and amount of contact, since it is the type rather than the extent of contact which influences attitudes: where contact has been of the pleasant, equal-status variety, attitudes are more likely to be favourable.

Tests were also carried out to discover if there were an association between favourability and such variables as length of residence in the town, age of interviewee, his occupation or education,[5] but none was found to be significant. One would hardly have expected length of residence in any one town to have been a decisive factor in racial attitudes as it might be, say, in the deep south of the United States, where racism is virulently widespread and therefore likely to rub off on to its long-term residents; whereas in

Table 11
Relationship of Attitude and Contact (N = 200)

	Great Deal		Fair Amount		Little		None		Total
	N.S.W.	*Vic.*	*N.S.W.*	*Vic.*	*N.S.W.*	*Vic.*	*N.S.W.*	*Vic.*	
Actively favourable (8, 7)	0	0	0	0	1	2	1	4	8
Tolerant (6, 5)	0	0	7	3	18	8	22	14	72
Slightly unfavourable (4)	0	0	4	2	12	8	11	18	55
Moderately unfavourable (3, 2)	0	0	3	5	4	14	13	14	53
Very unfavourable (1, 0)	0	0	0	0	2	5	2	3	12
Total	0	0	14	10	37	37	49	53	200

Eastville, for example, 46 per cent have at least tolerant attitudes towards Aborigines and only 4 per cent were very unfavourable.

There is a slight but not significant tendency for those who are favourable to be 21–29 years old rather than in the older age groups (no respondent was younger than 21 years of age); to have had some secondary or tertiary education; or to be employers or white-collar employees rather than manual workers.

An Eastville lawyer, who had spent most of his life in a wheel-chair following poliomyelitis as a child, had had professional contact with several Aborigines whom he had defended in court. He had an intense feeling of empathy for Aborigines as a group:

People always look on me as a cripple, not as an individual with endearing and unlikable characteristics; with abilities in some directions but not in others. They either avoid me, as being too divergent from the average to contemplate with equanimity, or they fall over themselves to be 'kind'. Often the help proffered is not what I need and is of an offensively superior kind. But this I could forgive if only they would stop putting me in a category, having fixed expectations as to my performance: 'One can't expect too much of him – after all, he's a cripple.' I'm excluded from all sorts of activities, treated as someone apart, almost non-existent at times, while at other times I'm smothered with an absurd amount of attention. All this erratic behaviour is accorded Aborigines, who are never sure how they'll be treated: fussed over paternalistically one day, ignored the next and always regarded as An Aborigine, not as just another fellow human being.

Community and Self-rated Attitudes

Respondents were asked to assess the attitude of their town and also what they believed to be their own attitude towards Aborigines (Questions 5 and 6). Replies were allocated over a five-point scale by the same panel of judges. As might be expected, no interviewee declared his own or his town's attitude to be very unfavourable. Percentages of those replies which were categorized as being either 'actively favourable' or 'tolerant' are listed in Table 12. Here ratings support the Aboriginal viewpoint that Eastville is the least and Westville the most propitious of the four towns in which to live. There is a significant difference (at the ·01 level by chi-square test) between Westville and Eastville both with regard to self-rated and town attitudes, while the difference between Northtown and Southtown is not significant for either attitude. There is a high correlation between a respondent's expressed attitude and his assessment of the town's attitude: those who profess to be favourable also regard their town as being favourable.

Table 12
Relationship Between Self-rating and
Rating of Towns

| | Favourable Attitude | |
	Self-rated %	Town %
Westville (N=50)	60	38
Northtown (N=50)	40	16
Southtown (N=50)	38	10
Eastville (N=50)	20	8

One of the reasons given for non-acceptance of Aborigines in Northtown was the fact that there was official discrimination in the Aboriginal favour: they are entitled to special benefits not accorded to whites. This white 'backlash' is beginning to make itself felt in various areas. A New Zealand researcher[6] reports some resentment in Dareton, New South Wales, to the secondary scholarships available only to Aboriginal students; the residents of Alice Springs have voiced similar opposition to special assistance to Aborigines; in Bourke, New South Wales, whites objected to the appointment of two Aboriginal field officers whose salaries were to be paid from the Australian section of Freedom From Hunger Campaign funds. A field worker with the Aboriginal Education Council in Sydney reported mounting resentment among country people affected by the rural depression toward Aborigines 'who were living on government handouts'.[7] As is being currently discovered in the United States, schemes which favour members of disadvantaged groups are likely to court the anger of the majority whites, who maintain that they are thus being discriminated against. The top American universities, for instance, are expected to reserve places for members of ethnic minorities and for women, which must inevitably mean that some white males will be excluded from limited quotas because they are WASPS. It is doubtful, however, whether such favourable discrimination engenders prejudice or whether it merely serves to exacerbate existing resentments.

Alcoholism was mentioned as the main bar to acceptance in Southtown, in Eastville it was lack of hygiene, and in Westville low educational level. The majority of respondents in all towns considered unfavourable white attitudes to be the result of deficiencies in Aborigines rather than to racial prejudice on the part of whites.

Relationship Between Various Measures of Attitude

The favourability score allotted by the judges was compared with respondents' self-rating and with the (necessarily subjective) rating of the interviewer. There was found to be a high positive correlation between all three, indicating a certain reliability in the rating method adopted (see Table 13).

Table 13
Correlation Between Attitude by Judges' Rating and Other Attitudinal Measures (four towns combined)

Self-rating	0·581*
Interviewer's rating	0·595*

* Significant at the ·01 level by chi-square test. (Contingency co-efficients have been standardized for comparative purposes.)

Stereotypes

During the interview, 52 per cent of all respondents mentioned attributes which they considered characteristic of Aborigines in general. It should be noted that these comments were unsolicited, and that all the attributes referred to were unfavourable. Some respondents mentioned more than one trait, others did not mention any. Table 14 indicates the number of respondents who referred to the trait concerned as being typical of Aborigines.

Table 14
Stereotypes

	Dirty	Drunken	Irresponsible	Inferior	Total
Eastville (N=50)	20	5	7	5	37
Westville (N=50)	9	4	3	4	20
Northtown (N=50)	10	10	12	7	39
Southtown (N=50)	9	11	7	4	31
Total	48	30	29	20	127

The term 'irresponsible' has been used to include such traits as lazy, unreliable and thriftless and the very frequently mentioned 'walkabout'. As has previously been remarked, many employers refuse to consider Aboriginal employees because they have had bad experience with two or three. They do not, of course, categorize white employees in the same manner.

There is a general tendency to attribute stereotypes to minority groups, since it is easier to generalize than to learn reasons for the conduct of individuals, and the four traits mentioned are those frequently ascribed to coloured minorities. The fact that there may be a kernel of truth in them does not prove that prejudice is not involved; it is more likely to be a sign that an unwanted trait in the respondent has been projected on to others and has become exaggerated in the projection. There is, too, an implied conflict of value systems in that Aborigines are seen to violate the conventional codes of cleanliness, work and sobriety. The frequent mention of lack of hygiene results partly from the poor living conditions of the majority of Aborigines of the four towns in the immediate past, and in some instances of the present, with lack of facilities for cleanliness. It also indicates the emphasis placed on hygiene in child upbringing in the white Australian society, where a child is made to feel guilty when he soils himself. Later, his burden of infantile guilt is transferred to others whom he wishes to punish as he was punished. The psychiatrist, Joel Kovel,[8] maintains that the racist has a sense of disgust at the body of a black person, based on a primitive fantasy: that it contains dirt that may rub off. He also draws attention to the fact that most groups which have been the object of prejudice have been called dirty: the Irish by the English, the Jews by the Poles, the Poles by the WASPS. This obsession with cleanliness was a striking feature with many of the white respondents in all four towns, and their willingness to accept Aborigines as friends was often followed by the rider, 'provided they're clean'.

The fact that the housing situation has improved substantially in all four towns over the last few years does not necessarily mean an instant diminution of prejudiced attitude, since this will persist for some time after the basic situation which shaped the attitude has been altered.

The visual element is apparent in Table 14: the squalor of reserve living was clearly visible to the residents of Eastville; excessive drinking in both Victorian towns frequently takes place on a public square in the centre of town, where it can be seen.

In the Western Australian study by Ronald Taft,[9] most traits selected from a given list as being typical of Aborigines were unfavourable: 'wasteful with money' came first, selected by 50 per cent of respondents, 'dirty and slovenly' by 28 per cent and 'drunken' by 26 per cent. Western[10] included in his survey the statement, 'The incorporation of Aborigines into our communities could well lower our standards of hygiene', to which an overall 21 per cent agreed.

Equality of Aboriginal Ability

Question 10 asked, 'Given the same opportunities, could Aborigines do as well as whites?' Affirmative replies, in percentages, are given in Table 15. Replies which appeared to be affirmative but which were immediately qualified were counted as negative:

'Yes, some of them could. Others wouldn't.'

'Well, that depends on what help they are given.'

'On the whole. But there are some of them who are just slackers.'

Table 15

Aboriginal Equality

	Affirmative %
Westville (N=50)	66
Eastville (N=50)	44
Southtown (N=50)	58
Northtown (N=50)	52
Total (N=200)	55

The difference between Northtown and Southtown is not statistically significant, but that between Westville and Eastville is (at the ·05 level by chi-square test). The Eastville Aborigines have until very recently been living in degraded conditions on the reserve and this appears to have been equated with inability to accept opportunities seemingly available to the entire community. Both Philp[11] and Western[12] included a similar question regarding inherent ability in their surveys, though they are not strictly comparable since each was limited in its application. Philp asked, on an Australia-wide basis, 'Supposing an Aborigine had the same kind of upbringing as you, do you think he could have learnt to do *your work*?' (italics added). The reply was 88 per cent in the affirmative. The question, however, implied specific job training. Western's statement was, 'Given the same opportunities Aboriginal *children* will do as well as white children' (italics added) to which he received assent from 95 per cent of his respondents in a city, and 86 per cent in a small town, both in New South Wales. This supports the contention, frequently expressed, that Aboriginal children where taken in hand early will make the grade, even though their parents' potentialities are most dubious.

Taft[13] asked of his Western Australian respondents an almost identical question, 'Given equal opportunities with whites, could Aborigines hold their own in every way?' In Perth 70 per cent of respondents agreed, and in two country towns 63 per cent, a percentage which lies midway between that of Southtown and Westville. The 1954 Gallup Poll, on an Australia-wide basis, asked a question similar to Philp's (as to whether Aborigines would be able to perform the respondent's job if given the same upbringing) and obtained a 90 per cent affirmative reply.

Disadvantages of Aborigines

Question 2 asked white respondents their view as to whether Aborigines suffered any particular disadvantage, and if so, of what kind. Replies were categorized into environmentally determined or inherent disadvantages, those who declined to categorize for Aborigines as a whole, and those who felt that Aborigines had positive advantages over the general populace (Table 16).

The difference in numbers of those who regard the disadvantages of Aborigines as being environmentally determined – that is, not of their own making – is significant (at the ·01 level) as between Southtown and Northtown. The

Table 16
Aboriginal Disadvantages

	Environmentally determined disadvantages	Inherent disadvantages	Positive advantages	Refusal to categorize	None	Don't know
Westville (N=50)	12	3	1	1	11	22
Eastville (N=50)	13	10	2	3	8	14
Southtown (N=50)	5	16	2	1	8	18
Northtown (N=50)	21	13	4	3	2	7
Total (N=200)	51	42	9	8	29	61

proportion who mentioned positive advantages enjoyed by Aborigines was greater in Northtown than in the other three towns, reflecting an awareness by whites of increased services to Aborigines in that town. However, overall numbers are far too small to draw any definite conclusions on this point. Those whose replies came under the heading of 'environmentally determined' made such comments as:

Most Aborigines seem to spend their lives going in and out of hospital. If you're crook all the time, how can you keep a job?

It's very hard for them to get jobs. They haven't much in the way of education and there's always a shortage of work for the unskilled.

Some of them live in such miserable hovels, they just can't compete with whites from a background like that.

It's just plain, miserable poverty that drags them down. What a lot of them could do with most is a good feed.

They don't get a fair go in this town. Everyone ignores them or else treats them like dirt.

Those who considered that Aboriginal disadvantages were inherent were apt to say:

They're just plain lazy – that's their trouble. I never had a fancy education either, but I've managed to make my way. A bit of elbow-grease is all that's needed to make good.

How can anyone do well when they fritter their money away, gambling?

It's drink that's their curse. There's something in the blood that makes them susceptible to alcohol – but they can't keep off the stuff.

If they'd just mix with the townsfolk, they'd be like us and things would be all right for them. The trouble is they're too cliquey. They stick in their own little world and don't seem to know or care what's going on around them.

Responsibility for Aboriginal Welfare

Official policy statements have been made from time to time[14] indicating that Aboriginal welfare (like other areas of welfare in Australia) is the joint responsibility of governments and private citizens. Questions 3, 7 and 8 were inserted to determine whether, in the public mind, action for improvement of conditions should be taken by govern-

Table 17

Increased Activity in Aboriginal Affairs

	Governmental		White		Aboriginal	
	N.S.W. (N = 100)	Vic. (N = 100)	N.S.W. (N = 100)	Vic. (N = 100)	N.S.W. (N = 100)	Vic. (N = 100)
Yes	61	57	52	56	5	5
No	16	17	22	14	71	82
Don't know	23	26	26	30	13	7
Unable to categorize	–	–	–	–	11	6

ments, by the general community of the town concerned or by Aborigines themselves. These three questions were asked in unrelated and not in alternative form, so that a respondent could have felt that more action was required on all three fronts simultaneously (see Table 17).

It is clear that substantial majorities both in New South Wales and Victoria consider that there should be more governmental and also more private activity in the Aboriginal field. But about one-quarter of all interviewees were unable to state whether more government or private aid was justified, adding as comment:

I've no idea what anybody's doing for them now, so I just couldn't say whether it's too much or too little.

Is there an Aboriginal Affairs office (or a voluntary Aboriginal body) in this town? I've never heard of it.

I suppose there must be something that could be done, but I haven't a clue what.

For those who favoured more action there was a differentiation between the role of non-government agencies on the one hand and of individual citizens on the other. For the government:

They should introduce some sort of public education campaign so that people would be more sympathetic to Aborigines and get off their backs.

Their pensions should be raised so that whole families can live decently – not like now.

Housing's always the bottleneck. A lot of them just can't afford to buy a decent house.

If they could get a bit more help with education, they'd be independent from then on.

The Aboriginal problem, as I see it, is one of jobs. If the government could provide them all with work, everything else would sort itself out.

The white citizens' support was to be more on an emotional and less on an economic level:

People just aren't friendly to Aborigines. They ignore them. Now, if every family were to invite one [Aborigine] home for dinner once in a while, it'd make them feel wanted.

Employers round here don't like offering jobs to the dark folk. But if they just gave them a chance they'd make good like the rest of us.

The trouble with our town is that too many are prejudiced against coloured people and regard themselves as superior.

The only significant difference of opinion (at the ·05 level) between the States was on the question of self-help among Aborigines, 82 per cent of Victorians and 71 per cent of those in New South Wales considering that Aborigines could not do any more to assist themselves. Those who felt they could do more suggested they should work harder, mix more with whites and become cleaner, thriftier and more reliable. An overall 8·5 per cent refused to place all Aborigines in the one category, stating that among Aborigines, as with whites, some could and some could not do more to improve their own conditions.

Aboriginal Community Centre

The desirability of an Aboriginal Community Centre in their town was acknowledged by 76 per cent of New South Wales respondents and by 81 per cent of Victorians (the difference between the two States is not statistically significant). However, many qualified their approval with the proviso that such a Centre should be under white direction.

Its main function was seen as the provision of adult education and household management classes, or as a general meeting place where white could assist Aborigine. Those who opposed the idea of a Centre did so on the basis that either there was not, or there should not be, a separate Aboriginal identity; or, alternatively, that property values near such a Centre would fall.

It is interesting to note that an Aboriginal Centre, with the implication of careful white control, is approved in all four towns, whereas the suggestion that several Aboriginal families be grouped together in town housing had been vehemently rejected in recent years in three of the four. In other words, an Aboriginal Centre is seen as a means of speeding up the acculturation process; group housing as a perpetuation of a separate Aboriginal identity.

Social Acceptability

Figures 1 to 5 represent the percentage of respondents in the designated town who would agree to admit part-Aborigines, Aborigines[15] or Italian migrants to each social-distance category. Figure 5 gives the totals for the four towns combined.

It is clear that Italian migrants were preferred over Aborigines in all towns, especially in the 'relative by marriage' category and there is a general, though not marked, trend for part-Aborigines to be more acceptable than Aborigines.

In Victoria more Northtown respondents claimed they were willing to have both part-Aborigines and Aborigines as relatives by marriage than did those in Southtown; in New South Wales more in Eastville than in Westville (both differences are significant at the $\cdot 01$ level). But in the other categories of social distance, there are no significant differences in acceptance.

Overall, 17 per cent of respondents would not accept a part-Aborigine as a family friend and 13 per cent would

Figure 1: Social Acceptability

WESTVILLE

(in percentages)

N = 50

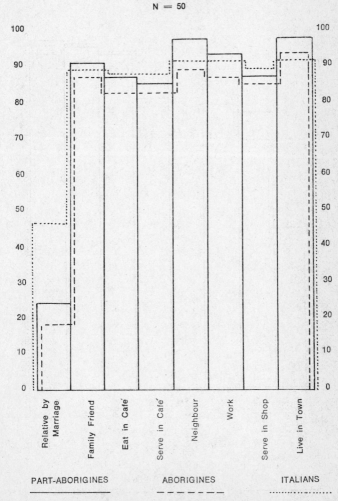

PART-ABORIGINES   ABORIGINES   ITALIANS

Figure 2: Social Acceptability

EASTVILLE

(in percentages)

N = 50

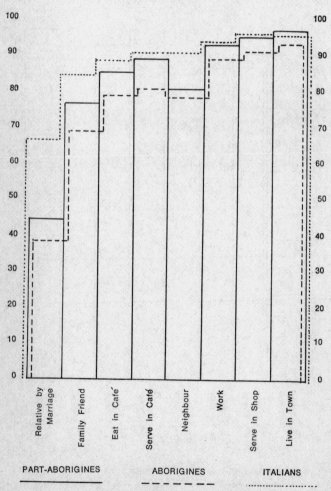

PART-ABORIGINES ———— ABORIGINES — — — — ITALIANS ··········

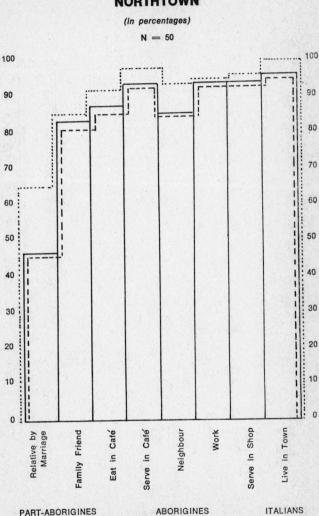

Figure 3: Social Acceptability

NORTHTOWN

(in percentages)

N = 50

PART-ABORIGINES   ABORIGINES   ITALIANS

Figure 4: Social Acceptability

SOUTHTOWN

(in percentages)

N = 50

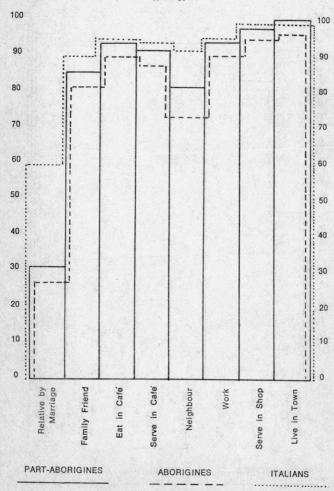

PART-ABORIGINES ———— ABORIGINES – – – – ITALIANS ....

Figure 5: Social Acceptability

FOUR TOWNS COMBINED

(in percentages)

N = 200

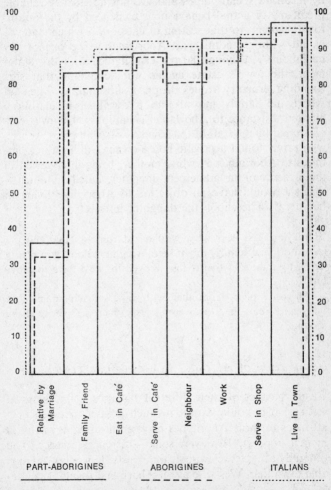

PART-ABORIGINES ———   ABORIGINES – – – –   ITALIANS ············

not accept one as a table companion in a café. These figures compare with 14 per cent and 11 per cent who would not accept Italian immigrants to these respective categories.[16]

That replies to the social-distance scale are influenced by idealized social values and are not necessarily reliable predictors of actual behaviour is evidenced by the Southtown response to that section of category 5 which states 'I would willingly admit part-Aborigines to be one of my neighbours'. Although 80 per cent agreed with this statement, the town's estate agents were emphatic that surrounding property values dropped substantially when an Aboriginal family moved into a dwelling, indicating a marked resistance to Aboriginal neighbours. This was corroborated by the staff of the Ministry of Aboriginal Affairs, who rarely found a private house-owner willing to let premises to Aborigines. A white mother, being interviewed in the presence of her adolescent daughter, stated quite firmly that she would have no objection to Aborigines living in her street. Whereupon the daughter interjected:

'But Mum, last year when you heard rumours that the —s [an Aboriginal family] might be moving next door, you nearly had a fit. You said that if they moved in, we'd have to move out!'

'Ah yes,' replied the mother, with some embarrassment, 'but I'd heard that the —s weren't very nice people to have around.'

Comparison of Attitudes Between Four Towns

Given the fact of their different histories and ecological settings, one would expect a much greater divergence in attitudes towards Aborigines between the four towns than in fact appears. However, some differences emerge. The generally accepted viewpoint that Eastville is a less favourable town than Westville as an Aboriginal living-place, despite the similarity of its social structure, is borne out on the whole by the survey. On the overall favourability scale Eastville ranks lower (though higher than the two Victorian towns); more Eastville residents considered Aboriginal disadvantages to be due to inherent factors; more thought Aborigines should provide greater self-help; fewer considered Aborigines to have ability equal to that of whites. But on self-rated and community attitudes, Westville's score was higher.

Reasons for the unfavourability of attitude in Eastville can also be inferred from the survey. Lack of acceptance in the town was attributed to lack of hygiene on the Aboriginal part, and 'dirty' was the stereotype most frequently mentioned. The influence of the very poor living conditions visible until recent years in the reserve and still visible in some of the sub-standard Aboriginal dwellings in the town is plain to see. The only point on which Eastville showed itself more tolerant than Westville was in its admission of Aborigines and part-Aborigines as relatives by marriage, though this may only signify a greater deference to general social values on the Eastville part.

Northtown may be beginning to react against special aid being available to Aborigines, but the reaction is too slight to enable this statement to be made with any certainty. In Northtown 8 per cent of respondents (the highest in the four towns) when asked if Aborigines had any especial disadvantages replied that, on the contrary, they had special advantages. Again, the reason most frequently given in Northtown for non-acceptance of Aborigines by the white community was that they had too much assistance. Northtowners showed themselves to be favourably disposed, however, by the large proportion who attributed Aboriginal disadvantages to environmental reasons.

Southtown scored lowest on the favourability scale, and indicated that alcoholism was the main bar to acceptance by the townspeople. Again, it was alcohol that was the most frequently mentioned of the stereotypes. As has been pointed out, drinking takes place in public places, and a small number of culprits are left to offend the town mores time and again.

Summary of White Attitudes

It is evident that the social distance between white and Aboriginal communities in the four towns studied is considerable, and is far greater than the idealized picture presented by the social-distance scale (Figures 1 to 5). One-quarter of all respondents displayed little or no interest in the Aboriginal situation (according to the interviewers' assessments), and only a handful showed keen interest. This is not surprising when it is considered that half the respondents had had no contact whatever with their Aboriginal fellow-townsmen.

Only 4 per cent of the interviewees were ranked as very favourable and 6 per cent as very unfavourable, the mildness of attitude of the majority reflecting lack of interest and contact as much as tolerance.

The influence of television was noticeable as being the principal medium of information on the Aboriginal situation. The fact that such programmes, however well presented, merely reinforce existing attitudes was made abundantly clear during the interviewing of Southtown whites. Immediately prior to this period, the Australian Broadcasting Commission had presented an hour-long current affairs programme on television on the overall Aboriginal situation, which many of the respondents had watched. Commented one interviewee, a shopkeeper:

It's a dam' shame what we've done to a fine people, forcing them to sit around helplessly, watching life pass them by. The government should provide them with decent housing and sanitation such as the rest of us have. It reflects on us all that Australian citizens have to live and bring up their kids in such degradation.

Another shopkeeper, living in the next street, had watched the same programme but had come to a different conclusion:

Did you see that TV programme the other night? Showed what a hopeless lot they are. Neither the government nor anyone else could possibly help them. There they sit on the ground all day, in the flies and dirt, breeding kids who are going to be no-hopers like their parents. You couldn't even *think* of them as being Australians, like us.

This accords with the research findings on the subject,[17] which have shown that mass communication rarely serves as an agent of attitude conversion (in the sense of reversal of opinion). The maximum effect that it can have is to create attitudes in regard to topics on which the individual had no previous opinion.

There is an inherent belief in the inferiority of the Aboriginal position (a belief constantly bolstered by reference to low material and social standards) which is sometimes transferred as belief in the inferiority of Aborigines themselves. All stereotypes mentioned pertaining to Aborigines (Table 14) were derogatory and Aborigines were both felt and seen to be in a continuously subordinate position.

A denial of separate Aboriginal identity was a feature of the survey and came both from those with favourable or unfavourable attitudes. Very often officials who were concerned with Aborigines would deny any differences between black and white, presumably on the assumption (not uncommon in Australia) that to be different is to be inferior; yet, at the same time, answers beginning 'Aborigines are . . .' and 'Aborigines should . . .' were freely given. In addition, it was not uncommon to juxtapose 'Aboriginal' and 'Australian': 'No, he's not an Australian, he's an Aborigine'! Only 4 per cent of all respondents declined to so categorize in reply to Question 2 (as to the cause of any Aboriginal disadvantages) and 8·5 per cent in answer to

Question 7 (that Aborigines could do more to help them-selves). This is in striking contrast to similar surveys over-seas which have been marked by an increasing refusal to apply stereotypes: in one instance, 59 per cent of an English sample declined to do so.[18]

In our survey 60 per cent of respondents were either slightly, moderately or very unfavourable.[19] This inherent prejudice, along with ignorance and lack of contact, makes it comparatively easy to stir up unease, bordering on panic, when any concerted movement of Aborigines into a town is thought to be imminent.* In three of the four towns the suggestion that several Aboriginal families be simultane-ously grouped together in the town had been seen as a threat by whites, and had been stopped by authority in deference to the wishes of the townspeople. Perhaps the low favourability rating of each town towards Aborigines suggested by respondents (Table 12) is not without sub-stance in fact.

Dr Kovel has suggested that most of us are 'metaracists' who 'acquiesce in the larger, cultural order which continues the work of racism'. In other words, people will adopt the attitudes which they regard as the norms of their reference group. Williams concurs with this view: 'The great majority of prejudiced persons carry prejudice at a low temperature . . . [which] reflects relatively passive conformity to taken-for-granted patterns prevalent in the social groups which give them their status and sense of belonging.'[20]

Long-standing habit gave conformity to the racial views of many of the country town respondents who tended to refer, paternalistically, to 'our' Aborigines ('I think we're pretty fair to our Aborigines'), and, among those favour-ably inclined, to distinguish between 'good Aborigines' and 'bad Aborigines': those who conform to prevailing white values and those who do not.

* In October 1972 one more white protest to Aboriginal group housing was made when local residents expressed fear that an Aboriginal workers' hostel in Dandenong, an outer Melbourne suburb, would cause a drop in surrounding property values.

Over all the discussions and rejoinders of the white section of this survey there hung the low cloud of adherence to the ideals of equality and fraternity, obscuring straight thinking and giving rise to what Gordon Allport has called 'the peculiar double-talk appropriate to prejudice in a democracy'.[21]

Notes

1. KATZ, D. and STOTLAND, E., 'A Preliminary Statement to a Theory of Attitude Structure and Change', in KOCH, S. (ed.), *Psychology: A Study of A Science*, vol. 3, New York, 1959, p. 428.
2. The wording was that used by RONALD TAFT (in 'Attitudes of Western Australians towards Aborigines', *Attitudes and Social Conditions*, Canberra, 1970), to whom acknowledgement is made.
3. PARK, R. E., *Race and Culture*, Glencoe, Illinois, 1950.
4. WILLIAMS, ROBIN M. jun., *Strangers Next Door*, New Jersey, 1964.
5. *Correlations Between Background Factors and Attitude to Aborigines* (four towns combined).

Length of residence	0·307*	n.s.
Age	0·301	n.s.
Occupation	0·226	n.s.
Education	0·179	n.s.
Amount of contact	0·148	n.s.

(*Contingency coefficients have been standardized for comparative purposes.)

6. Personal communication from Mr John Stanton, University of Auckland.
7. News item on Australian News Bulletin, Australian Broadcasting Commission, 23 July 1971.
8. KOVEL, JOEL, *White Racism, A Psychohistory*, London, 1970, pp. 81–4.
9. TAFT, R., op. cit.
10. WESTERN, J. S., 'The Australian Aborigine: What White Australians Know and Think About Him – A Preliminary Survey', *Race*, vol. 10, no. 4.

Words or Blows

11. PHILP, H. W. S., 'Prejudice Towards the Australian Aborigine', unpublished Ph.D. thesis, Harvard University, 1958.
12. WESTERN, J. S., op. cit.
13. TAFT, R., op. cit.
14. See statement issued by Commonwealth–State Conference on Aboriginal Affairs, Perth, July 1967; also statement by the Hon. W. C. Wentworth, M.H.R., Minister in Charge of Aboriginal Affairs, to the Fifth National Conference of the Australian Council of Social Service, Brisbane, 1968.
15. It will be noticed that a differentiation has been made on the social-distance scale between Aborigines and part-Aborigines, whereas previously both terms have been covered by the word 'Aborigines'.
16. Western Australian figures (TAFT, R., op. cit.) for part-Aborigines in these two categories were 25 and 20 per cent respectively. In a similar study of social acceptability of Aborigines in New South Wales (JENNETT, CHRISTINE, 'Racism and the Rise of Black Power in Australia', M.A. qualifying thesis, University of N.S.W., 1970), 12 per cent of white respondents had negative attitudes towards Aborigines (or part-Aborigines) moving next door, while 27 per cent had a positive attitude towards a family member marrying a full or part-Aborigine.
17. KLAPP, JOSEPH T., 'Mass Communication, Attitude, Stability and Change', in SHERIF and SHERIF (eds.), Attitude, Ego-Involvement and Change, New York, 1967, pp. 297–309.
18. BANTON, M. P., White and Coloured, London, 1959, p. 37.
19. A massive survey of English attitudes towards race in 1963 disclosed that 27 per cent were prejudiced. Criteria, however, were so different from those used in the present study that the figures are scarcely comparable (ROSE, E. J. B. and DEAKIN, NICHOLAS, Colour and Citizenship, Oxford, 1963).
20. WILLIAMS, ROBIN M. jun., op. cit., p. 200.
21. ALLPORT, G. W., The Nature of Prejudice, New York, 1958.

Chapter Thirteen

Aboriginal Situation and Attitudes

Needless to say, the characteristics and attitudes of the four Aboriginal communities summarized here are broad generalizations and do not purport to reflect the viewpoint of all Aborigines, some of whom have interacted with whites extensively and have acquired a similar outlook. However, they do apply to a substantial majority of Aborigines studied, whose similar history and present social situation have given rise to a remarkable sameness of attitude.

Social Organization

The big majority of Aborigines, though geographically situated in the four towns, still regarded themselves as part of the regional kinship group from which they originated, and which for the majority was in the surrounding area. This contributed both to mobility and to restriction on movement: any emigration from the area, for example, in search of employment or housing, was likely to be of a temporary nature, because there were strong ties to the region of origin and the relatives and friends it contained; and only within this region were primary relationships formed. Migration within the area is continuous since such relationships are reinforced both by periodic social meetings of a regional nature at which attendance is consistently high among both old and young, and on which great value is placed; and by ceaseless visiting for varying periods. Men and women who had previously lived on the river bank near Northtown or on the reserve near Eastville and who had since moved to comfortable houses in the town frequently extolled the 'good old days', where physical conditions were appalling but group integration was high and there was much sharing. A couple with school-age children recalled how they would sit around at night on the river bank and yarn and sing and tell stories; and how, when there was sickness or acute poverty, food and care were always available without the asking. And now the sense of tight-knit community had gone. An Eastville woman reminisced about the former reserve, five miles from the town, where the whole district would foregather each Sunday for church, a meal with relatives and an afternoon's visiting and gossip.

Now I come into town of a Sunday and meet my Mum and my four sisters and we walk up and down the streets together and have a bit of a chat while the children play. But if it's raining, we just can't all be together. We're a big family when you count in the three generations and the in-laws, and we don't fit into one house. All our homes are just too small. If only we had a hall or some place to go!

Many with this attitude were not old enough to have developed a generalized nostalgia for the past, nor had they forgotten the negative aspects of shanty life, but implicit in their viewpoint was the recognition that reserve living had fulfilled the need to belong (in a limited community) in a way that life in the town did not.

Formal communication within the family appears slight, at least judged by middle-class standards, and parents often have little idea of the whereabouts or viewpoint of children. Yet basic attitudes are transmitted from one generation to the next and employment and education opportunities are sought by those whose parents have long been seeking them (though not always successfully). Permissiveness from both generations prevents overt clashes and, when offspring in their turn produce children, the support of the grandparents, and particularly of the maternal grandmother, can be taken for granted in even the most difficult circumstances.

Cultural

Traces of the traditional culture are slight and do not play a major part in Aborigines' lives, yet small phrases of the vernacular or of traditional medical remedies only half believed, are used to bolster group identity. An awareness of shared experience is also a strong bond and there is a reaching out to learn something of this experience, especially on the part of younger people. An adolescent girl in Victoria, after hearing a series of lectures on Victorian Aboriginal history, commented, 'Now, at last, I feel I have roots'.

In Northtown there is still interest in the (derived) traditional art of carving emu eggs. One elderly Aborigine makes his living by so doing and is instructing a young man as an apprentice. In Westville an old-age pensioner makes an auxiliary income by selling hand-made boomerangs. Interest in both Northtown and Southtown was high in a Melbourne Aboriginal group which travelled round the countryside giving a 'corroboree': songs and dances based on those of tradition. This gradual reaching out towards a traditional culture which these part-Aborigines had never known is one manifestation of a slowly growing feeling of pan-Aboriginalism. It also reflects the changing attitude of the major society towards what is known as 'primitive' art, which is now more positively valued than it has been in the past.

Aboriginal Agencies

Specific institutions for Aborigines are provided by the major society in recognition of the disabilities which Aborigines suffer for social and historic reasons. Periodic statements as to 'the withering away of the State', that is, to an eventual decline in the provision of special Aboriginal services, are greeted with some derision by Aborigines, who see the officers of these agencies as being in comfortable and ever-expanding jobs. In New South Wales the traditional attitude of hostility to authority was strong, and the local welfare officer was foisted with the blame for misfortunes which could not logically have been his fault. Services provided by the Board were largely of a patching-up kind, of assistance to those in distress.[1]

In Southtown government assistance had gone further, in offering home ownership and opportunities for advanced education, job training and a specialized health service. This had reinforced the already emerging two-class social system in what had originally been an unstratified community, a system based not so much on education, occupation and economic criteria (as in the general community) but on acceptance of the values of the wider society. In Northtown the rate of acculturation was faster and expectations higher, since the services of private and government agencies had been available for longer, and the background of the Aboriginal people concerned disposed them more towards self-assertion; hence the more pronounced stratification of the community. In particular, those who accepted the concept of steady employment as a desirable goal were inclined to look down on those who did not, and to cut them off socially.

There is a tendency on the part of Aboriginal agencies, whether government or private, to cater for the more successful Aborigines with whom it is easier to make contact and who are genuinely interested in opportunities for upward mobility; and to regard the rest as beyond help. This is why increasing government services have brought increasing stratification, with the more successful viewing the rest as a barrier to social acceptance of the Aboriginal group as a whole. Though officers of the government agency in all four centres were aware of the dangers of paternalism, and efforts were made to consult with their charges and to involve them in activities, there was a wariness of approach, an understandable gulf between the highly educated and socially aware purveyors of services and their far less socially knowledgeable charges. The psychiatrist, Mindell,[2] has commented on such assistance programmes to ethnic minorities: 'Underneath we are afraid of their [the minority's] increasing strength and assertiveness: we are threatened by it.'

Attributes of Poverty

The proportion of those whom Hylan Lewis called the 'clinical poor' – those too ravaged emotionally by poverty and deprivation to adapt to new opportunities – is small, though it undoubtedly exists. But many of the characteristics of a 'sub-culture of poverty'[3] are present throughout the four communities. Included in these are low wages, high unemployment, poor housing, overcrowding, and a sense of community; together with a low level of organization, feelings of marginality, helplessness, dependence and inferiority. The crucial trait of such a sub-culture is the 'lack of participation in the institutions of the larger society',[4] evidenced by such items as rejection of education and lack of membership in voluntary associations. These traits are exhibited in large measure by our four communities.

Separate Identity

Notwithstanding the emergence of stratification in the two Victorian Aboriginal communities, the feeling of group identity within them, as in the New South Wales town, is still high. A young Aboriginal girl attempted explanation: 'Aboriginalism is not a way of life or a racial difference only. It's just something we all feel – a state of mind.' The 'state of mind' is maintained by two very effective mechanisms of social control: gossip and public opinion. Social exclusion – observed particularly in Northtown – of those who do not conform to the group's norms, is used to devastating effect. This was apparent on one occasion when a group of women met together to make toys to be sold on a street stall. Another Aboriginal woman, obviously in the 'lower class' category, entered, anxious to join the group in their work and chat. Her presence was entirely ignored by the rest: she was not given any materials with which to work, nor was a single word addressed to her. After two hours of wretched silence, she gave up her attempts to cross the friendship barrier and departed.

There was no apparent desire on the part of individuals to integrate socially with whites, though any act of discrimination towards one member was immediately noted and bitterly resented by the whole community. An extreme sensitivity towards criticism, real or imagined, was apparent. Anything that could be construed as a derogatory remark or action from a white was so construed. A young woman in a doctor's waiting room in Eastville, noting that another (white) patient who had arrived later was called into the surgery before she was, commented bitterly: 'See what I mean. I was here before that white woman, but us dark people always have to wait at the end of the queue.' It was pointed out to her that there were in fact two doctors sharing the one waiting-room and that it was the other doctor who had called in the white patient. But it is doubtful whether she listened to this explanation.

This super-sensitivity is obviously an attitude born of experience: of discrimination in housing and employment, of constant items in the mass media which stress the marginal position of the Aborigine in all parts of the country. In Southtown great bitterness was aroused when an officer of the Ministry of Aboriginal Affairs was reported in the press as adjuring doctors to send their Aboriginal patients bills, the implication being that Aborigines were not in the habit of paying their medical expenses. Aborigines felt they were constantly under attack by those in authority (though such was not the intention of the officer concerned) and were angry, yet frustrated by their defencelessness, their lack of hitting power.

Employment in the four communities was usually not regarded as an integral part of everyday living nor was industriousness considered a positive value. There are numerous hurdles to overcome before employment can be obtained. First the (white) employment officer and then the (white) employer have to be aproached, either or both of whom could have prejudice against Aborigines.[5] In any case jobs are very scarce for men in three of the four towns and are virtually unobtainable in all four for women and juniors. Even when a job is secured, the attitude of one or more workmates could imply a distaste for coloured people; or a freezing-out process might take place where an Aboriginal employee feels himself isolated from the general coterie of workers. The job itself is not likely to bring any satisfaction, being a dull, repetitive one which whites are loath to take and which brings no prospect of change or advancement. Within his own community little kudos is obtained from getting a better-than-average job: on the contrary, envy and scorn often ensue. In short, the linkage of employment with upward social mobility which is a normative value in the white society does not necessarily apply in the Aboriginal one.

Lengthy exclusion from the major society has had the effect of excluding Aborigines from a knowledge of its processes, making the achievement of even simple aims almost impossible. Lack of social awareness brings a spirit of unreality as to how society works and how it can be manipulated to individual advantage. What might be termed an 'urbanized cargo cult' mentality ensues: seeing whites frequently accomplish objectives by manipulation of social institutions to their own advantage, Aborigines feel that, by banding together and expressing their desires with great emotionality and only a little practical effort, these will eventuate. When nothing is achieved, the feeling of powerlessness, of the futility of attempting to change the *status quo*, brings about what is known as Aboriginal 'apathy'.[6] There were many whites in the towns surveyed who, with only primary education, or even incomplete primary education, were yet successful in business, in voluntary organizations and in local government and held in high respect by the general run of townsfolk. But these people had all been brought up within the general society and had a knowledge of its workings, which Aborigines lacked. This lack gave rise to a distorted and unreal appreciation of how societal institutions operate. Seeing themselves always on the outside, Aborigines were convinced that whites in general knew how to manipulate these institutions for their own benefit, while they themselves constantly experienced rejection. Lack of social knowledge has also the effect of making aims unreal: the dividing line between what is a feasible and an unfeasible scheme is often blurred, and attempting the impossible adds to frustration and to the conviction that the cards are stacked against the coloured person. To a certain extent this want of knowledge is offset by officers of Aboriginal Affairs departments whose job it is to mediate between Aborigines and employers, social welfare departments, housing bodies and the like. But this again is seen by the Aborigine as placing himself in a dependent role, always having to approach a white for assistance.

Members of minority groups who have constantly experienced discrimination have only a limited number of reactions open to them. If they accept the image of inferiority bestowed on them by the major society they can either be submissive, accepting their Aboriginality (for example) as evidence of inferior status; or they can withdraw, pressured by self-hatred or expediency. If the means of success are not available, the aspiration to succeed will vanish. A retreatist of this sort will not engage in thievery, for instance, because he has assimilated the cultural prohibitions against such behaviour, or else has been unsuccessful as a criminal. Therefore retreatism has become his only possible adaptation. This may show itself, and sometimes does so among Aborigines, in the form of alcoholism, dubbed by society as 'deviant' behaviour. But anti-social behaviour is logical for those whom society has rejected.

Those minority group members who refuse to accept permanent inferiority may plump for integration, to be brought about (in the Aboriginal instance) by black organizations, working for equal opportunities within the general framework of society; or else by avoidance of the white society. The assumption of inferiority will be negated with a Black Action movement, stressing that 'Black is Beautiful' and that black people are and always have been achievers. This is likely to bring in its train some measure of voluntary segregation: the suggestion, for instance, that the Northern Territory should become a black State, owned and controlled by Aborigines, to which whites might well be attracted by its different lifestyle and the superiority of its institutions to those of the major society.[7]

Perhaps the most strikingly consistent feature of the four Aboriginal communities was their positive evaluation of Aboriginal identity, which shows no sign of diminishing, even among the young. Those who had been well accepted in the major society on an individual basis (such as those prominent in sport) were resentful of the less than whole-hearted acceptance of Aborigines as a group, and of the marginal position which they felt themselves to occupy.

Needs and Aspirations

During the course of the survey it became clear that there was a concensus within the four Aboriginal communities as to certain needs which related both to underlying principles in the handling of Aboriginal affairs and to such specifics as education, employment and health.

Aborigines of the four towns were highly sensitive to anything that singles them out as special beneficiaries, thus emphasizing their inferior position. It is still necessary to have specialized Aboriginal agencies or Aboriginal sections within a general agency, to accord with the realities of cultural difference and to act as liaison between Aborigines and the rest of the community. But there could well be a second criterion of services provided, namely, that of need. Scholarships, now sometimes accepted with reluctance, would be welcomed if they were part of a generalized scheme based on economic need-cum-ability, and this would obviate the small but growing white protest against favourable discrimination towards Aborigines. Similarly, nursing services centred on a geographic area for all citizens would imply no stigma and arouse no envy.

Aborigines were often aware, also, that the difference for an individual between success and failure, of keeping to a course of education or employment or of relinquishing it, is frequently in the quality of the personal relationships involved. They are used to relating to others as a whole person and not in the depersonalized relationships to which we are accustomed, especially in urban living. As one of them commented: 'We see people as people – not as a doctor or a teacher or a boss.'

Sympathetic teaching staff at a High School near Southtown, who were always available for discussion and showed real interest in their charges, made the Aboriginal children feel wanted and a part of the school. Motivation for achievement was thus provided and the students responded well. Similarly, employers who had an attitude of respect and high expectation towards Aboriginal employees exemplified the theory of 'self-fulfilling prophecy': their expectations were usually realized. Seen in this light, Aboriginal 'failure' sometimes turns out to be white failure – a failure in human relations, or a lack in understanding.

This lack of understanding also frequently manifests itself when a white official assumes that upward social mobility is the motivating force in Aboriginal lives, since the official himself has been socialized in the ethos of 'getting ahead', and knows no other. Aboriginal affairs officers who make this assumption are bound to experience frustration, and their disappointment then becomes manifest to the Aborigines concerned. There is an (understandable) reluctance on the part of such officers to deal with Aborigines who are not so motivated. But assistance to the relatively successful has the effect of sponsoring a small élite, while leaving the majority, the so-called multi-problem families, without adequate support. On their part, Aborigines know it is useless to explain to whites in general that strong emotional ties to the black community, often necessary to mental health, prevent their availing themselves of opportunities which would isolate them in a white void.

In recent years, emphasis in Aboriginal affairs has been on the encouragement of young Aborigines to continue in their education and to undertake job training: both necessary provisions. But Aborigines are beginning to demand that attention be given to additional aspects of education in the wider sense, not directly related to employment, but having an important bearing on all facets of Aboriginal life. As has been pointed out, one of the most striking differences between white and Aboriginal adults is the ignorance of the latter as to the workings of society and its institutions: areas of national, State and local government; legal, welfare, health and educational services. Combined with this ignorance is a lack of knowledge of a citizen's rights, both civil and legal. Adult 'civics' courses for both men and women, with both legal and procedural emphasis, are necessary if Aborigines are to feel less frustrated and to become independent in this generation. Leadership and human relations training must also be available on demand. Even more necessary are opportunities for Aborigines to plan and direct programmes to fulfil the aspirations of their own communities (as distinct from the aspirations of whites *for* Aborigines). For some little time to come the support of white specialists will be required for such projects but it is imperative, if they are to achieve any measure of success, that they be left to Aboriginal direction. Two of many such programmes which, in a short time, have already proven themselves are the Aboriginal Health Service and the Aboriginal Legal Service, both with headquarters in Sydney. Each was the result of a group of Aborigines taking action to respond to a felt need. Each operates with the assistance of white professionals. But the lawyers and medical practitioners concerned see their role as a supportive one and it is a group of Aborigines who run the services, thus providing basic legal and medical care to a community which had previously been deprived of it by estrangement from the major society and by poverty.

It has been found that members of an ethnic minority who identify positively with their own group are likely to have more inter-racial contact and to integrate more easily,[8] and that this positive ethnocentrism can unite minority members in efforts to improve their position. There is a very real interest (and an equally real ignorance) on the part of Aborigines in New South Wales and Victoria in their history, both pre- and post-contact, and a desire to learn more of the traditional culture and the situation of Aboriginal groups other than their own. The lectures that were provided on Victorian Aboriginal history have been enthusiastically received by those who are usually reluctant to display enthusiasm, and interest was high both in young and old. Talks on Aboriginal culture and history could lead to discussion of the present-day situation and to the articulation of group problems. From this point the next step would be the formulation of plans and their implementation by the Aboriginal group concerned, who could call on government finance and on support by specialists where required. But, in order to stand any chance of success, they must be black plans and policies, assisted but not manipulated by whites.

Aborigines often expressed the desire to be employed in groups, where they would cease to feel socially isolated. Far from causing an apartheid mentality, grouping engenders work stability by making the social background of the workplace more congenial and thus facilitating integration into the world of white workmates from a position of ease and confidence, should the individual Aborigine so desire. 'Voluntary separatism' is clearly not the same as imposed segregation.

An Aborigine working in the Victorian Ministry of Aboriginal Affairs proposed that, in addition to the existing services for job placement, provision of sheltered workshops be made in Aboriginal areas for those whose previous history and emotional state preclude them from taking and retaining a job in the regular workforce. Those with a record of constant or sporadic unemployment (a substantial number in the communities studied) could find part-time employment in a congenial atmosphere among members of their own group. The social interaction thus available would act as stimulant to longer periods of work and less itinerancy.

Anxiety was frequently expressed over alcoholics, as to what could or should be done to assist and treat them. Unless some provision is made for referral for treatment, 'regulars' will continue to be charged by the police, goaled for a short term, released to repeat the syndrome and even incur the emulation by adolescents of such parental behaviour. A small community with many personal problems and limited resources finds it increasingly difficult to cope with these deviants, and also with a number of middle-aged and particularly of elderly men, with a life-time of non-employment or very erratic employment behind them, whose behaviour is considered anti-social even by their own community. Social care is needed for them by the provision of men's homes, either for Aborigines only or on a racially mixed basis, in country areas where they will not be completely cut off from kin.

And finally, contrary to general belief, it was found that Aborigines did not accept their low level of ill-health as natural and inevitable. Underneath the stoicism which is shown to the outside world was a constant anxiety, especially regarding children, whose suffering and sometimes early death was most deeply mourned. Only the 'culture of silence' in which Aboriginal people are accustomed to live, a product of the whole situation of paternalism and powerlessness, prevented their crying out in anger at this, the ultimate inequality.

Social Distance

The feeling of social distance and the actual social separation between black and white communities was great, even where both lived side by side in the same small town. This is no doubt due to the physical separation of one from the other during the long years when most Aborigines lived on reserves; the inferiority of the Aboriginal position with regard to employment, housing, education and income; and the fear of difference on the part of whites, exaggerated by the traditional adherence to the positive value of 'homogeneity'. Evidence of this separation was reflected on the Aboriginal side in the seemingly low inter-marriage rate and the reluctance to pass for white, even where this was feasible. On the white side it was evidenced by the 50 per cent of the sample who had little or no contact with Aborigines, of whom some were even surprised to learn that there were Aborigines living in their town. Though Aborigines did not seek interaction with whites, nor did acceptance in the general society necessarily bring prestige in their own community, they none the less resented non-acceptance and were highly sensitive to any sign, real or imagined, of slight.

Separation, together with prejudice, has also strengthened the feeling of constant pressure from without: to a white employer one might not be acceptable, to a white house-owner not wanted as tenant; in any case, a white employee or tenant, if available, would always be preferred. What contact there was with whites was of an unequal kind, with health and education officers, with middle-class members of Aboriginal civil rights groups which, far from bridging the gap, served to exacerbate it. Though transistor radios and television were bringing some sort of fairytale window on the world, they were not automatically giving Aborigines a wider view of the general society or making them an integral part of it. Government agencies for Aborigines, which might be regarded as a means of bringing the two communities together, often have the reverse effect;

as instruments of a superordinate society, they act as a catalyst for anti-white resentment.

The distance between black and white communities, not surprisingly, gives rise to very different viewpoints as to the present Aboriginal situation. Whites, with a certain vague optimism, felt that in course of time Aborigines would recognize the obvious superiority of white values, particularly of upward social mobility and the steps necessary to achieve this end, and would adopt them. An Aboriginal community centre was seen as an instrument of deculturation rather than of re-acculturation: that is to say, a place in which Aborigines are trained to acquire the behaviour and thought patterns of the major society rather than reinforce the traditions of their own.

The continuing socio-economic inferiority and separation of the Aboriginal community has called forth adaptive mechanisms similar to those displayed by other ethnic minorities living in poverty; among them the strong feeling of group identity, with stress on acceptance of the individual by Aboriginal society as a whole. Though there was some sign in the four towns of part-acculturation bringing with it less emphasis on sharing or on retaining the almost static social position of the rest of the Aboriginal group, these values nevertheless were still prized and were strong motivating forces to action, or to inaction. On the whole, the feeling of interdependence of fate which Aborigines share with each other prevails over the desire for success in the major society.

The Aboriginal attitude to their separate identity was clear-cut and unambiguous, stemming as it did from shared history and present-day experience, cultural differences and frequent rejection or threat of rejection by whites. This separate identity was considered a positive value necessary to group survival. White attitudes were ambivalent: prejudiced whites in particular were the first to reject the very possibility that there could be cultural differences within the Australian community; or, if such differences were conceded, they were seen as detrimental to both the group concerned and to society as a whole. And whereas Aborigines were not averse to maintaining the social distance between the two communities, members of the major society (even those with unfavourable attitudes) usually considered that integration or assimilation should take place through further acculturation on the Aboriginal side.

Nowhere was the divergence of view greater than on the question of the present and future Aboriginal situation in Australia as a whole. By and large, whites saw the Aboriginal position as inferior, but not disturbingly so (though the better-informed and more sympathetic had more comprehension of the status gulf between black and white communities). They considered that, by means of various agents of social change, or by means unknown, it was improving all the time. Aborigines saw their situation as being chronically depressed and showed no confidence in the future. Which viewpoint does an objective assessment of the situation favour?

To support the optimists is the steady change for the better in public attitudes since the early days of white settlement. The original habit of regarding the Aborigine as little better than the native fauna, or of not regarding him at all, has given way to a growing awareness of his claims on Australian society and of his subordinate position within that society. This has been reflected in an increase in public expenditure on Aboriginal affairs which in 1970–1 was to the order of $44 million, and to a steady decrease in discriminatory legislation, until only Queensland and the Northern Territory still offend in this regard. But this is cold comfort to an Aborigine who is faced with racialism, particularly of a paternalistic kind, in administration and in his personal contacts in daily life. Furthermore, for members of a minority group of generally low status, mere tolerance is not enough. It is easy for an educated white of liberal persuasion to be tolerant. It is not so easy for him to accept as equal the social 'outsider', to view him as an individual as well as a member of a particular group, and to feel for him the concern which he automatically accords those whom he considers peers.

The usual indices of status and social position within a community are occupation, education, housing and health – all measurable commodities. It is doubtful whether the Aboriginal situation is improving in any of these aspects. A conservative estimate of the need for standard houses for Aborigines is around ten thousand, with a thousand more families being added to the waiting list each year. During the financial year 1971–2, Federal and State funds combined would probably house between six and seven hundred families. This falls far short of the annual growth and does not make any inroads at all into the huge backlog. If the New South Wales figures are held as criterion, the retention rate for Aboriginal students in secondary schools is rising at a very much slower rate than the white, so that the disparity between the two communities (as with housing) is actually increasing. The employment pattern shows a continuation of poorly-paid, low-status occupations, with a high degree of unemployment. In a submission to the Senate Standing Committee on Social Environment, the Commonwealth Department of Labour and National Service stated that it had only been able to place 6,500 Aborigines in jobs in 1971 out of a total of 22,000 who sought employment assistance.

Nowhere is the gulf between black and white so great as in the field of health. All surveys that have been carried out in Aboriginal areas have indicated a significantly higher morbidity and mortality rate for children and adults. There is no indication in any area of a substantial and lasting improvement: in Central Australia the position has steadily deteriorated with the Aboriginal infant mortality rate rising from the already enormously high rate in 1969 of 89 deaths per 1,000 live births in the first year of life to 182 per 1,000 for 1970–1.[9]

Nor is there comfort in the legal situation, where social disorientation and discrimination before the law give rise to a disproportionate number of criminal charges against Aborigines and an even more disproportionate number in penal institutions.[10] In New South Wales in 1970, for example, according to figures supplied by the New South

Words or Blows

Wales Police Commissioner, 40 per cent of people convicted of drunkenness were Aborigines, who comprise 1 per cent of the population. Again, there is every indication of a worsening situation.

In the light of all the evidence, present despondency and lack of confidence in the future seem not unreasonable Aboriginal attitudes.

Notes

1. Since the time of the survey, the Welfare Board has been abolished and its functions taken over by the Department of Child Welfare and Social Welfare.
2. MINDELL, C. E., *Pine Ridge Reserve Bulletin*, no. 6, December 1968.
3. LEWIS, OSCAR, *La Vida*, London, 1965, pp. xxxix–xliv.
4. LEWIS, OSCAR, *A Study of Slum Culture: Background for La Vida*, New York, 1968, pp. 11–12.
5. The First Assistant Secretary (Employment and Training) Department of Labour and National Service, giving evidence before the Senate Standing Committee on Social Environment on 8 May 1972, stated: 'There is absolutely no question but that some employers ... do not favour employing persons known to be Aborigines.'
6. As Freire has so aptly expressed it: 'Hopelessness is a form of silence, of denying the world and fleeing from it.' FREIRE, PAULO, *Pedagogy of the Oppressed*, New York, 1968, p. 60.
7. These broad categories of response have been suggested by ROSE, PETER I., *They and We*, New York, 1964.
8. WILLIAMS, ROBIN M. jun., *Strangers Next Door*, New Jersey, 1964, p. 296.
9. Non-Aboriginal rate for the Northern Territory as a whole in 1966 was 19·5 per 1,000.
10. Detailed figures for Western Australia, South Australia and Victoria are given in EGGLESTON, ELIZABETH, 'Aborigines and the Administration of Justice', unpublished Ph.D. thesis, Monash University, 1970.

Conclusion

The dichotomy between black and white attitudes on fundamental issues concerning Aborigines is, in reality, far greater than the findings of such a limited survey would suggest. Likewise, changes necessary to combat the gross inequality of the Aboriginal position must be of a far more radical kind than those which have been outlined in the preceding chapters.

Overt harshness and cruelty towards Aborigines have gone; no longer are they shot, poisoned and despised. In this sense, white attitudes of the past have changed radically. Yet, in another sense, they have hardly changed at all. The desperate clinging to an ideal of Anglo-Saxon homogeneity remains, a homogeneity which in fact has not existed since the first days of black–white contact and is most unlikely to exist again. Rapid communication and transport, the constant migration and interaction which modern societies bring in their train will ensure that Australia becomes steadily more heterogeneous. But will the disparate parts eventually be swallowed up in one homogenized whole? This 'melting pot' theory has long since been shown as false in the United States. As fast as some individuals and groups assimilate, others come to take their place: migrants from other countries or resident ethnic groups who strengthen their ethnicity and assert their right to a separate identity, a separate culture.

Nor does such multi-racialism inherently bring social strife. Mauritius and the Hawaiian islands (to name but two examples) have maintained their cultural diversity for generations, with marked absence of friction. Social differences can be equally or more divisive. The potential for friction between those with greater or less access to power and resources, or between political groups of diametrically opposed philosophies (even though these are all white) is at least as great as that between the races. We have amassed more than our share of xenophobia on these shores and seem willing to accord equality only to those who promise not to be different – though different from what is never made clear. It has been said that human dignity is a matter of social permission; such permission has been entirely absent from white attitudes to Aborigines, partly because their traditional culture was too alien from our own for us to comprehend. Even now, when the social sciences have torn aside the veil of ignorance, we are still apt to reject the Aboriginal culture as inferior, overlooking the fact that our own society would become more congenial if it offered more intellectual variety and stimulation, the cultural richness of inter-group living.

The present position of Aborigines does not just result from the sum total of individual attitudes, nor even the summation of attitudes and historic events. It is also a political question, of the distribution of influence and power and, ultimately, of community resources. Many whites of liberal persuasion are now ready to accept guilt, to admit to a racist past and to make amends, and will most earnestly urge more public expenditure on housing and welfare services. But the notion of real equality for Aborigines is as yet too radical a departure from past concepts to gain acceptance: not that it has been tried and found wanting, but simply that it has never been tried. Only a handful of whites are ready to press for a radical change in the situation of the disadvantaged. Most would be content with a small up-grading, bringing in its train some improvement in health, welfare and education – but not too much. But more fundamental thinking is required from liberal opinion if we are ever to proceed beyond this piecemeal approach. Racial inequality is not an isolated problem, but is rooted in the social and economic structure of our society. It has frequently occurred in other countries that an ethnic group has been able to raise its social position by climbing on the shoulders of another group, more recently arrived, as the Maoris have done with the Pacific Islanders. But for Aborigines, the only way to get off the bottom rung is to eliminate that rung altogether. Otherwise, special benefits and privileges will be resented by the white poor, and race relations will be exacerbated, not improved. The question we face is both attitudinal and economic. Why, in a wealthy, industrialized country can we not build adequate housing for all, maintain a steady rate of employment and find funds for education? The racial crisis challenges the entire society's capacity to redirect its resources on the basis of human needs rather than of material production. Aboriginal advances must not be made at the expense of the alienated, the outcast and the poor of whatever colour, who should be joint beneficiaries in programmes of social change. A linkage between the disadvantaged groups would assure them more voice, more resources and more equality.

In Australia we usually go through four stages in dealing with social problems. In the first instance, we deny that they exist or, if they do exist, then to nothing like the same extent as in other countries. (Just as, in discussing one's personal faults, they are nothing like as serious as those of other people. In fact, on reflection, they become positively endearing.) When the evil becomes too great to be ignored, we resort to excuse and explanation: such problems are unique to this country and their insolubility is likewise unique. At this juncture we decide that certain reforms will, in fact, have to be made, and the enthusiasts band together to pressure the power structure accordingly. In course of time, government will cede to popular persuasion and put the matter in the keeping of full-time 'specialists', the problem being thereby considered solved. The enthusiasts move on to other areas, convinced that the situation is being guided and guarded by a benevolent bureaucracy, under the supervision of politicians of goodwill. We have just reached this stage in Aboriginal affairs and are in danger of falling back into the complacency so dear to us. Administrators, on their part, develop a commitment to their carefully devised programmes and, even where these are not producing the desired results, will patch them up with more resources, rather than scrap them entirely as admission of error.

And Aborigines, who are on the receiving end of these plans and ministrations, are they also complacent, do they consider more welfare the solution to their ills? To speak with any group in any part of Australia is to receive a resounding 'No' to what would be regarded as an absurd question. Equally absurd is the suggestion that all Aboriginal action to express discontent and strike at its root causes must be attributed to sinister white 'stirrers', when it is obvious that no group in history has been content to remain permanently on the bottom; and Aborigines feel they have been there long enough.

For many years a mindless 'policy' ordained that Aborigines should be scooped up from their dwelling-places and cajoled or forced on to settlements and reserves, in areas that were not economically viable and where the level of services was scarcely adequate to maintain life. That such institutions could only end in disaster was not, apparently, foreseen. The present low socio-economic position of Aborigines, together with their inability to compete with the white man because of lack of self-confidence and self-respect, can all be attributed to this enforced separation. Now, a curious paradox has arisen. The early policy of separation was purely a white man's concept, in which Aborigines were not consulted. Quite recently, however, they have begun to demand a voluntary separatism for either some of their communities or some of their community services. From this they believe that a new life-style will stem, based on the community action and group decision of the traditional society, combined with the technical aids of modern living. Such group action is not a stubborn clinging to the past; a refusal to change with the times. Wherever minority groups have seen wealth and material ease alongside them, they have reached out for their share; and now, even the more remote of Aboriginal groups are aware of white Australian life-styles, and desire a certain measure of integration by affluence. It is with such concepts that the Black Power movement is concerned: the freedom and resources to determine the destiny of the black community. Employment, housing and education are included in these demands, together with equality before the law and compensation for land usurped. In varying Aboriginal areas of Australia there has come about a spontaneous desire for change, an impatience with chronic disadvantage. Black communities are formulating and administering their own plans, based on their expressed needs. Schemes for housing, for medical and legal services, schools and pre-schools, administered by Aborigines but with white technical and economic assistance, are springing up. To date there have been both attitudinal and practical blocks preventing Aborigines from availing themselves of general community services: they may have no transport to take them to a hospital, no money to pay the attendant charges. Even more difficult to overcome than these disabilities are psychological disadvantages, less apparent but more insidious, which stem from a lifetime of social separation: problems of using a 'phone to make a hospital appointment, of finding one's way through a maze of buildings, of communicating with a doctor of a different class and colour, and fear of reprimand for alleged inadequacy.

In the capital cities especially, an Aboriginal intelligentsia is developing, people who have a compartively high level of education and who are anxious to use it for the benefit of their own community. Small country towns and remote settlements have not this advantage and may require still further resources to generate their own development: courses in human relations or in leadership will assist Aboriginal groups to run their own affairs with expertise and without the friction inherent in small, inter-related groups. Funds may be needed to institutionalize such community development by enabling the employment of full-time Aboriginal administrators, responsible only to their own people. To facilitate these changes will be to avoid the mistakes made by many of the War Against Poverty Programmes of the United States in the 1960s which failed because they were planners' programmes of white, middle-class experts and lacked the very essentials (such as job-training and employment) for which black communities were crying out.

The recently formed Black Panthers and other Black Action groups in Australia have tended towards dramatic statement to satisfy their need for militancy: a not unreasonable retaliation for all the hurt and misery which they have suffered. But, in practice, they have a positive approach which seeks to build up their own communities by self-help. White aid for such schemes is acceptable – even essential – provided initiative and leadership remain in black hands. Black action on such lines is the surest way for Aboriginal communities to regain the sense of purpose and direction which once they knew and to experience for the first time a fair measure of equality with whites.

Aeschylus once said that learning comes through suffering. Small wonder, then, that Aborigines have much to teach. If we will listen to just demands and follow Aboriginal leadership in Aboriginal affairs, if some element of White Power will but cede to Black, we shall be met with words, not blows and, in due time, heal with the balm of empathy the wounds of a racist past.

Appendix I

Questionnaire to Whites

1. What contact have you had with Aborigines?

   A great deal
   A fair amount
   A little
   None

2. What, in your view, are the main disadvantages (if any) under which Aborigines live at present in............?

3. Could the government do anything further to improve conditions?

4. How do you think Aborigines would respond to these improvements?

5. What is the general attitude of whites in.............. towards Aborigines?

6. What is your attitude towards Aborigines?

7. Could Aborigines do more to help themselves? If so, what?

8. Could the citizens of................do more to assist Aborigines? If so, in what way?

9. Do you think it a good idea to have an Aboriginal community centre in Eastville/Westville? If so, what would you like such a centre to do?

   OR

   Do you think the Aboriginal community centre in Northtown/Southtown is a good idea? What would you like the centre to do?

10. Given the same opportunities, could Aborigines do as well as whites?

Words or Blows

11. Respondent's (a) Sex: Male   Female
                (b) Age: 20 – 29
                         30 – 39
                         40 – 49
                         50 – 59
                         60 – 69
                         70 and over
                (c) Length of residence in town:
                (d) Occupation:
                (e) Educational level:

12. Attitude (as rated by interviewer):
    Actively favourable
    Tolerant
    Slightly unfavourable
    Moderately unfavourable
    Very unfavourable.

Appendix II

Social-distance Scale

According to my first feelings: I would willingly admit part-Aborigines, Aborigines or Italians (considered as a class and not just the best or the worst ones you have known) to one or more of the classifications below.

Place ticks in the squares that show your answers.

	Part-Aborigines	Aborigines	Italians
A relative by marriage			
A family friend			
To eat at the same table as me in a café			
To serve food to me in a café			
To be one of my neighbours			
To work alongside me on my job			
To serve me in a shop			
To live in (my town)			

Any other comments:

Index